PENGUIN PASSNOTES

Twelfth Night

Stephen Coote was educated at Cambridge and London University. He was Director of Studies and Head of English at a London tutorial college, and is currently General Editor of Penguin Passnotes. He has written two other guides in this series, *Wuthering Heights* and *Macbeth*.

PENGUIN PASSNOTES

WILLIAM SHAKESPEARE
Twelfth Night

STEPHEN COOTE, M.A., PH.D.

PENGUIN BOOKS

Penguin Books Ltd, Harmondsworth, Middlesex, England
Viking Penguin Inc., 40 West 23rd Street, New York, New York 10010, U.S.A.
Penguin Books Australia Ltd, Ringwood, Victoria, Australia
Penguin Books Canada Ltd, 2801 John Street, Markham, Ontario, Canada L3R 1B4
Penguin Books (N.Z.) Ltd, 182–190 Wairau Road, Auckland 10, New Zealand

First published 1984
Reprinted 1985

Made and printed in Great Britain by
Richard Clay (The Chaucer Press) Ltd, Bungay, Suffolk
Filmset in Monophoto Ehrhardt by Northumberland Press Ltd, Gateshead

*The publishers are grateful to the following Examination Boards for
permission to reproduce questions from examination papers used in
individual titles in the Passnotes series:*

*Associated Examining Board, University of Cambridge Local Examinations
Syndicate, Joint Matriculation Board, University of London School
Examinations Department, Oxford and Cambridge Schools Examination
Board, University of Oxford Delegacy of Local Examinations.*

*The Examination Boards accept no responsibility whatsoever for the
accuracy or method of working in any suggested answers given as models.*

Contents

To the Student

This book is designed to help you with your O-level or C.S.E. English Literature examinations. It contains an introduction to the play, analysis of scenes and characters, and a commentary on some of the issues raised by the play. Line references are to the New Penguin Shakespeare, edited by M. M. Mahood.

When you use this book remember that it is no more than an aid to your study. It will help you find passages quickly and perhaps give you some ideas for essays. But remember: *This book is not a substitute for reading the play and it is your response and your knowledge that matter.* These are the things the examiners are looking for, and they are also the things that will give you the most pleasure. Show your knowledge and appreciation to the examiner, and show them clearly.

Introduction: Background to Twelfth Night

A fine performance of *Twelfth Night* is one of the most delightful experiences the theatre can offer. The play is sophisticated and moving. It is also very, very funny.

This rich combination of moods shows Shakespeare at the height of his powers. He took an appealing and fairly well-known story, re-fashioned it with all the skill of an experienced playwright, and then lavished on its retelling great poetry and superb comedy. There is also much memorable characterization.

As we watch the play unfold, we are aware of its constantly changing moods. While we never lose sight of the absurd plot and want to laugh, yet, as the characters become more deeply entangled, so we become aware of suffering and poetry. Love, upon which the play centres, is shown to be a powerful and beautiful force, but one which can drive people to absurdity and extremes. In *Twelfth Night*, there is real pain on the road to happiness.

This variety of mood is crucial. The play moves swiftly from rapture to slapstick, aided by a variety of characters. We see Orsino, a rare and exotic connoisseur of passion; and Viola, fresh, faithful and strong. The Lady Olivia has turned her back on love, but suddenly discovers its desperate, convulsive power. The 'low-life' characters add variety and comment: Sir Toby and Maria, in their raucous and earthy delight, are touching as well as funny; Sir Andrew Aguecheek is absurd but pathetic. Malvolio, 'sick of self-love', the would-be courtier and lover, the 'madman' and, finally, the one rejected character, comments on all these themes in the play.

The themes are principally concerned with the nature of such highly important matters as love and truth. That Shakespeare chooses to present them in a comic way does not detract from their seriousness.

In *Twelfth Night*, the final truth of love lies in the happy marriages of Olivia to Sebastian, Viola to Orsino, Sir Toby to Maria. They have grown out of illusions: Orsino's illusions of romantic passion, Olivia's unnatural withdrawal from the world. Only when these illusions – which have pushed some characters to the edge of reason – have been worked through, when Viola can throw off the last illusion and prepare to reveal herself as the woman she really is, can happiness and truth prevail. Yet this is only part of Shakespeare's final effect. *Twelfth Night* closes with Feste's song, a beautiful yet melancholy lyric which reminds us perfectly of the rare and precious world that Illyria is.

Synopsis

The play opens in the court of Orsino, Duke of Illyria. Music is playing and an atmosphere of heady, romantic passion pervades. Love is praised as imaginative in the highest degree (ll.14–15). We learn that the lady Orsino loves is called Olivia. A messenger Orsino has sent to her returns and tells him how Olivia has turned her back on the world and vowed to mourn her dead brother for the length of seven summers (ll.26–32).

Against reason, Orsino interprets this favourably. If Olivia loves her dead brother so strongly, how much more will she love Orsino in the end. Intoxicated by such hopes, the Duke sweeps off 'to sweet beds of flowers'.

The second scene shows us the survivors of a shipwreck. A sea captain tells Viola they have landed in Illyria. She, meanwhile, mourns for her brother whom she supposes to be dead. The Captain comforts her by saying he saw the young man – we later learn that he is Viola's twin, named Sebastian – clinging to the wreckage (ll.11–17). He may well be safe. Viola, a little comforted, asks if the Captain knows Illyria. He does. He tells her about Orsino, informing her that he is a bachelor and in love with Olivia (ll.29–34). He then describes Olivia's mourning. Viola wishes to serve the lady in secret and, when told this is impossible, replies that she thinks she can trust the Captain and so she will tell him her other plan, which is to disguise herself and serve Orsino as his page (ll.48–62). She will sing and entertain him. The Captain agrees to keep her secret.

After such high romance, we descend to low life. We meet Sir Toby Belch, a drunken and earthy older relation of Olivia's. (Although Sir Toby is Olivia's 'kinsman' and calls her 'niece', he is not necessarily her uncle. 'Niece' had a less precise meaning in Elizabethan England than it has today.) We see at once that Sir Toby is a loose-living rogue and, even if we are only reading the play, we gather something of his character from his surname. He is being berated by Maria, Olivia's maid, for his late nights and disorderly conduct (I, iii, 3–15). We learn of his ludicrous companion Sir Andrew Aguecheek whom, upon his entry, we see at once as a foolish fop. The idea that Olivia will marry him is utterly absurd. He begins to realize this, but Sir Toby persuades him to stay for another month. The couple exit in comic high-spirits.

Viola has disguised herself as a boy, calling herself Cesario. As a page, she has won Orsino's complete confidence (I, iv, 13–14). Also, although he does not realize this, she has fallen in love with him. He, meanwhile, is so impressed with Cesario that he orders him to go and woo Olivia in his place (ll. 15–18). Cesario's youthful charm is likely to succeed where Orsino has failed. The scene closes with Viola bewailing the bitterly ironic position in which she finds herself.

We are then introduced to another main character – Feste, Olivia's jester or clown. After a great display of wit to Maria, during which he suggests that Sir Toby loves her (I, v, 1–28), we see him trying to comfort Olivia. Feste has been absent without leave and can reasonably expect Olivia to be angry. Olivia is in mourning and Feste tries to lift her mood of sorrow and depression, with some success (ll. 29–67). But when Olivia turns to Malvolio, her steward, for his opinion of Feste, Malvolio's dislike of the clown is clear and he denigrates him in front of Olivia (ll. 78–84). Feste will not forget this. We learn from Olivia that Malvolio is 'sick of self-love'. Maria then announces the arrival of a young man. We suspect it is Viola in the guise of the pageboy Cesario. Malvolio is sent to turn her away for Olivia wants no messages from Orsino. Sir Toby enters, drunk. He quickly departs, followed by Feste (l. 133). Malvolio has been unsuccessful in ordering Cesario off and Olivia agrees to see him (l. 157). She veils her face as Viola enters. We see Viola forcefully arguing Orsino's love, and her manner stirs Olivia's interest. Olivia lifts her veil, revealing her beauty (l. 223). Viola generously admires her beauty and continues to state Orsino's love with ever more evocative poetry. Olivia is adamant she will have none of him but she does suggest Cesario might return. Viola refuses the present Olivia offers and leaves, somewhat angered by her hard-heartedness. Alone, Olivia recognizes the onset of love (ll.278–87). Taking a ring from her finger, she gives it to Malvolio, telling him to run after Cesario. She pretends that the ring is his and that she is returning it as unwanted. She will give her reasons to the youth if he will return tomorrow (ll.295–6). Olivia is in love and desperate to see Cesario again. The situation is both comic and touching.

Viola's brother, Sebastian, has indeed been saved from the wreck. He reveals his identity to his friend Antonio, who begs to stay with him (Act II Scene i). Sebastian twice tries to dissuade him and expresses grief at what he believes to be his sister's death. The two men part, but Antonio follows Sebastian after a short soliloquy in which he expresses his intense friendship for him.

Viola and Malvolio meet. Malvolio haughtily drops Olivia's ring at her feet, and, when left alone, Viola shows how she suspects Olivia has fallen in love with her, thinking she is truly the boy Cesario. She recognizes the symptoms of love in Olivia and realizes how dangerous her disguise is (II,ii,27–32). She also realizes, to her sorrow and our amusement, the irony of the love knot which has been tied between herself, Orsino and Olivia.

Sir Toby and Sir Andrew Aguecheek are up late, drinking. Feste joins them, and as the stream of wit and the effects of the wine raise their spirits, Feste is called upon to sing (II,iii,30). The song makes them melancholy and they decide to cheer themselves with a round or catch. This revelry brings out Maria, who tells them to be quiet (l.70). Olivia has probably called Malvolio, but they are too drunk to care. Malvolio indeed now enters in his nightgown to create a wonderfully ridiculous moment, but Sir Toby pulls rank on him and Malvolio is forced to leave. He threatens to report Maria to Olivia. Maria and the drunkards are angered and vow their revenge. Sir Andrew threatens to challenge Malvolio to a duel. Maria has a better idea. As her handwriting is almost identical to Olivia's, she will forge a love letter from Olivia to Malvolio (ll.148–54). She knows he will fall for this, make himself ridiculous, and so provide them with much entertainment.

After this comic interlude, Act II Scene iv is deliciously melancholy. Orsino demands the song Feste sang the night before, and, while the jester is being summoned, he discusses with Viola the nature of love (ll.15–41). She intimates that her love is for Orsino, but because of her role and disguise she cannot confess it openly. Feste then enters to sing his beautiful but melancholy lyric and so create one of the high points of the play (l.50). When he has gone, Orsino orders Cesario back to Olivia after discussing the sadness of rejected love. The pathos of Viola having to hide her feelings here is both ironic and moving.

Act II Scene v is superbly comic. Sir Toby, Sir Andrew and Fabian – a new character – are sent by Maria to watch Malvolio as he struts through the garden, soon to find her letter. They overhear Malvolio fantasizing about marriage to Olivia and the contempt with which such a marriage would allow him to treat Sir Toby and Sir Andrew. There is much comedy here as the observers barely restrain their indignation. Eventually, Malvolio finds the letter and reads in all its complexities the expression of Olivia's passionate love for him. His bursting pride and soaring hope, and his belief that his daydreams have been fulfilled are wonderfully absurd. He will indeed appear before Olivia as her lover and, as the letter suggests, in yellow stockings with cross-garters (ll.159–66). The observers are delighted at the success of their ruse. We should notice, however, that Malvolio's love for Olivia is in some respects a caricature of the loves of the nobles in the play.

Viola and Feste meet and, after a witty exchange, Feste successfully begs money from her (III,i,42). She encounters Sir Toby and Sir Andrew as Feste departs. Olivia then enters. She sends the others away so that she may be alone with Viola who, dressed as Cesario, seems to her to be the man she loves. Yet again Viola tries to impress on Olivia the ardour of Orsino's love. Olivia is interested only in her own passion for Cesario. She confesses to her ruse with the ring and Viola responds with generous pity (l.120). For Olivia, this gives hope of love. She vainly struggles to dismiss Cesario from her affections and, after a complex exchange in which each suggests the other is not what she appears, Viola shows a little anger (ll.140–41). Olivia confesses the depth of her passion in an aside (ll.142–53). Viola then departs, leaving Olivia hoping she will return.

Sir Andrew is determined to leave Illyria. He has seen Olivia express more affection for Cesario than she ever has for him (III, ii, 4–6). He is tricked by Sir Toby into thinking she has done this only to awake his 'dormouse' valour. Sir Andrew should fight the youth. He agrees to this and leaves to pen his challenge. Sir Toby thinks the duel will be excellent entertainment. Maria enters to inform Fabian and Sir Toby of the imminent arrival of Malvolio, who is dressed in exactly the absurd way her letter advised.

Between this scene and Malvolio's courtship of Olivia we meet Sebastian and Antonio again. Antonio has caught up with his friend and Sebastian welcomes him (Act III Scene iii). Antonio tells of the danger he is in. He is an old enemy of Orsino's (ll. 26–38). He gives Sebastian his purse, having recommended the Elephant as the inn at which they should stay. They part, Sebastian to view the town.

Olivia has sent after Cesario and is waiting for him in a state of great excitement. Malvolio enters to pursue his absurd courtship. Olivia has already been told by Maria that Malvolio is 'possessed' and his ridiculous performance, in which he quotes the contents of what he thinks is her letter, serves to suggest that this might almost be true. A servant then announces Cesario's arrival (III,iv,57). Olivia, all excitement, asks for Sir Toby to look after Malvolio. To Malvolio, this is yet further proof of Olivia's love for him. The letter had instructed him to be obstinate to Sir Toby, and here is his chance to be so. Sir Toby and Fabian enter. Malvolio tries to slight them, but they treat him as if he is mad and he sweeps off. They pursue him, threatening to lock him in a 'dark room'. This was the usual treatment for lunatics in Elizabethan times.

Sir Andrew then enters with his absurd challenge prepared (l.141). He goes to search for Cesario. Sir Toby recognizes that if the duel is to take place at all he must encourage it himself. Sir Andrew's feeble letter is useless. As Olivia enters, he and Fabian depart.

Olivia at once expresses her bitterness at Cesario's coldness towards her (ll.197–201). The depth of her love is clear as she presents a portrait of herself and begs Cesario to return the next day (ll.204–208). It is a brief, painful interview and Olivia leaves shortly after.

Viola is left no time in which to react. Sir Toby enters and presents a terrible and, to the audience, ridiculous picture of a valiant Sir Andrew Aguecheek bent on revenge. Viola is utterly confused. She neither knows Sir Andrew nor can imagine how she may have insulted him. She is clearly very frightened. Farce here carries a note of terror. Sir Toby then drags in the quaking Sir Andrew and gives a broad description of his opponent's monstrous valour. He too is terrified. In an absurdly comic moment, these most reluctant duellists are brought together. They are about to draw when Antonio also enters (l.301). He, of course, confuses Viola for Sebastian. No sooner has he drawn his sword to save his friend than the Officers come in to arrest him. Such wild coincidence and farce are gloriously funny, but Antonio is bitter when he begs for the return of his money (in other words the purse he had given to Sebastian). Viola does not understand. She has never seen the man before. She offers to lend what little money she has, but Antonio – still thinking she is Sebastian – rounds on her for her ingratitude (ll.356–61). He names Sebastian in his passionate outburst, and the Officers, thinking him mad, take him away. Viola, however, is breathless with the hope that the Sebastian he has named is her own brother, still alive.

Sir Toby, Sir Andrew and Fabian remain. They call Cesario a coward and vow future vengeance.

There is an exchange of wit between Sebastian and Feste. Sir Andrew Aguecheek enters and, mistaking Sebastian for his sister, strikes him (IV,i,23). Sebastian strikes him back, much harder. Feste goes off to tell Olivia of the fight. Sir Andrew threatens to sue. Sebastian and Sir Toby draw their swords just as Olivia enters (l.43). Horrified, she orders Fabian and the two knights to leave and then, rushing to protect Sebastian – whom she thinks is the Cesario she loves – bids him go with her. Sebastian, now utterly amazed by the people of Illyria, willingly accompanies this strange and beautiful woman.

The next scene presents the taunting of Malvolio. Feste disguises himself as a priest and, urged on by Sir Toby, bates the 'madman' in the darkened cell where they have locked him. The scene is funny; it is also, particularly to a modern audience, cruel. Only after a lengthy revenge does Feste finally agree to bring Malvolio a light and paper and ink so that he may write to Olivia (IV,ii,118). Here indeed is revenge.

In contrast, the last scene of the fourth Act is rapturous and comic. Sebastian can barely believe how he has been swept into such a tangle of intense love. Indeed, he can hardly believe he is sane (IV,iii,8–21). But there is no time left to him in which his questions can be answered. Olivia enters and rushes the man whom she still believes to be Cesario to a priest. She thinks that she has finally won Cesario's gratitude and hastens to the priest so that her beloved may engage her and plight his faith in the sight of heaven.

Act V is one long, glorious unravelling of the plot. It opens with Feste refusing to let Fabian see the letter Malvolio has written from his madman's cell. Orsino then enters, ready to encounter Olivia, whom he sends Feste to bring (l.39). Viola, who has accompanied Orsino, recognizes Antonio as her rescuer the moment he enters, still under arrest. Orsino recognizes him too. Antonio is his enemy, a man who has fought successfully against him (ll.48–56). Antonio explains his relationship with Sebastian and, still mistaking Viola for him, berates her for her ingratitude. Viola, of course, can neither understand nor believe what Antonio is saying.

Olivia enters, adamant about her refusal of Orsino. He, bitter at his rejection, and with a strong suspicion that her affections are directed towards Viola (still disguised as Cesario) threatens to kill his page as an act of revenge (ll.115–29). Viola, deep and steadfast in her love, willingly accepts this. She prepares to leave with Orsino. Olivia, naturally unable to understand Cesario's behaviour, calls out after her. How can her 'husband' run away like this? The priest enters and is told by Olivia to witness the vows she and Cesario, as she believes, have just sworn. Orsino is bitter at what he sees as Cesario's treachery. Has he really become engaged to the woman Orsino himself loves?

Sir Andrew Aguecheek now limps in, followed by a drunk Sir Toby and Feste. Both knights have been hurt in their conflict with Sebastian and no sooner is Sir Toby helped off to bed than Sebastian himself enters, apologizing profusely for striking Olivia's kinsman (l.206).

Identical twins – Sebastian, and Viola disguised as Cesario – are now on stage. The scene is one of absolute confusion. Sebastian turns gratefully to his friend Antonio and then sees his sister (l.223). We witness a wary but increasingly joyful recognition of brother and sister, Viola finally agreeing to throw off her disguise when all the details of the past have been tested. Sebastian turns to Olivia, his future wife, while Orsino turns to the pageboy he now knows to be Viola. They plight their troth, but the mention of Malvolio reminds the whole company of him (l.273). Feste comes in with his letter which shows Malvolio to be both sane and quite justifiably upset. As Malvolio is sent for, Olivia proposes the double marriage, at her own cost, of Orsino to Viola, and herself to Sebastian. This is willingly accepted.

Malvolio now enters in high dudgeon (l.324). Olivia explains that she did not write the letter, that the handwriting is Maria's. She says that Malvolio has indeed been badly treated but that he will be the judge of his own case and punish the offenders. Fabian explains the true position and suggests that there is right and wrong on both sides (ll.353–9). Feste, however, points with bitter triumph to the revenge he has had. Malvolio stalks out, vowing revenge in his turn. Orsino hopes he can be persuaded to a better temper, but, in the meantime, he will look forward to hearing the whole story and preparing for his marriage. The company of happy, united lovers leaves. Only Feste remains to sing the beautiful but melancholy closing song.

Scene by Scene Analysis

ACT I SCENE i

We are first introduced to Orsino, Duke of Illyria. He is suffering from the extreme pangs of love and hopes the music he is hearing will ease him. He listens to it and luxuriously compares it with the smell of violets in the breeze. For a while the music does bring relief. Soon, however, the effect wears off and Orsino orders the musicians to cease playing. He declares that his love is as bottomless as the ocean. It can swallow everything and yet it devalues everything. Love ('fancy') is the most inventive and imaginative force in the world (ll.14–15). We see at once that Shakespeare presents romantic love as greedy, fickle yet deeply poetic. It takes people over utterly. We must understand this to appreciate the play.

Orsino's courtiers suggest the lovelorn Duke goes hunting. He makes a pun on the word 'heart' and we learn the name of the woman he is in love with: it is Olivia (l.20). We see how powerfully she affects him but, with the arrival of Valentine, we learn more. Olivia is in mourning for her dead brother and has resolved to shut herself off from the world for seven summers. She will have nothing to do with Orsino. The Duke's love is to be unrequited. He, however, is sure he will eventually win her. Since she loves her brother so strongly, how much more will she love Orsino when she finally relents (ll.34–42).

The first scene is short but exactly sets the tone of ardent, aristocratic love, desire and suffering. But, since Orsino has already said that such love is changeable, we may wonder if he himself will change and love another woman. And what of Olivia? Will she really reject all men for so long?

ACT I SCENE ii

We are next introduced to Viola, the woman Orsino will love and eventually marry. She has been shipwrecked on the shores of Illyria and is worried about her brother whom she fears may have drowned. The Captain comforts her by saying he saw someone like Sebastian clinging to the wreckage. He is rewarded and then tells Viola how he was born only three hours away from where they now stand. He adds that the ruler of the country is Orsino. Viola learns that Orsino is a bachelor and in love with Olivia. We also learn that Olivia's father has died (l.37). She is all alone in the world.

Viola first declares she will serve Olivia, and then, when told how difficult this would be, that she will serve Orsino instead. She asks the Captain to keep her secret, for what she has in mind is to disguise herself (ll.56–60), entertain the Duke, and bide her time.

Of course, it is all a preposterous combination of coincidence and wild, unlikely planning. Shakespeare intended it to be. We are not in a real world, but a comic and poetic one. 'This is Illyria, lady'; Illyria is a place of comedy, poetry and disguise.

ACT I SCENE iii

Illyria is not just a place for lovelorn aristocrats. It would be insipid if it were. Viola and Orsino both move us and make us smile. Sir Toby Belch and the handmaid Maria are down-to-earth people who make us laugh. We recognize Sir Toby at once: he is a fat and carefree drinker who is invariably guzzling deep into the night. We shall learn more of Maria later, but we hear now of Sir Toby's drinking. Sir Andrew Aguecheek is another knight, a foolish spendthrift and a quarreller. He is not at all the scholar Sir Toby says he is; rather, upon his entry, we see a tall, thin, witless creature with long, lank hair. We know him at once to be a figure of fun. He would like to be a lover. He has come to Illyria in the hope of wooing Olivia. He would also like to be a wit, but, as Maria proceeds to make a complete fool of him, we see that he knows nothing at all about women and is too stupid to see that Maria's wit is all at his expense. We begin to see Maria as a shrewd and lively woman who has her feet firmly on the ground.

Sir Andrew is depressed when she leaves and in his conversation with Sir Toby Belch we see how completely foolish he is. Toby can mock him, live off his money and even persuade him that he has a chance of wooing Olivia. Put so baldly, this makes Toby Belch appear no more than a confidence trickster. In part, this is what he is, but he is also so vigorously alive – and Sir Andrew Aguecheek is such a nincompoop – that we laugh outright and are wholly on Sir Toby's side. We revel in his energy, wit and roguishness. (A good director will make Sir Andrew appear truly ridiculous as he boasts about his accomplishments, his wit, his drinking and dancing.) Sir Andrew Aguecheek thinks he is a virile man of the world, but compare him with Orsino. Both are in love with Olivia. Both, as it happens, stand no chance of winning her hand. But whereas Orsino is passionate and brooding, a man of deep, poetic and changing moods, Sir Andrew Aguecheek is a feeble creature, quite incapable of high, romantic passion. He is no lover but a fop. We laugh at him and yet, as we shall see, we also feel slightly sorry for him. Sadness – what the Elizabethans called melancholy – is never far below the surface of this play, and it is part of Shakespeare's genius that he moves so easily between the touching and the funny, what makes us sad and what makes us laugh.

ACT I SCENE iv

We return to Orsino's court and so move from farce to high comedy. Viola, now in boy's attire and renamed Cesario, has become the Duke's page. It is typical of Orsino's impulsive nature that he has taken very suddenly to his new servant. What we may see on the stage – but are not explicitly told until the end of the scene – is that Viola has fallen deeply in love with him.

Left alone, Viola and Orsino talk. The Duke has told his new servant all the details of his love and he now asks Viola to court Olivia for him. In the first scene we learned how difficult this is, for there we saw Valentine unsuccessfully returning from the same mission.

Notice how the verse deepens the tone, how it suggests the grandness of passion. It also suggests its violence. Viola is told to be 'clamorous and leap all civil bounds'. And what is she to do when she has gained admittance? Study Orsino's reply carefully, for the language tells us much. He is sending Viola to 'act' his woes, while the 'passion' of his love does not only mean his emotion. 'Passion' is an Elizabethan word for a play. The characters are not what they seem. They are play-acting. The idea of things not being what they appear, of illusion and reality, is suggested here; and the Duke's words make it clear in his next speech that Cesario, being as pretty as a girl (which, of course, is what Viola really is), will have a far more favourable effect on Olivia than his own 'grave aspect'.

It is all deliberately and delightfully confusing. Viola's final, rather desperate outcry confirms this: she is in love with Orsino.

Reduced to its bare bones, what has happened is this: Orsino in his lonely passion has taken strongly to his new page. Cesario, though he does not know this, is a woman. The Duke asks his trusted 'boy' to court the woman he is in love with and does not realize that Cesario – the woman in disguise – is deeply in love with him. How easily this could descend into farce. But it is not farce because the poetry makes the passion so effective. Certainly we smile, but we are also moved. Indeed, in Viola's brief declaration of her love, and hence of the dreadful position in which she finds herself, there is just a trace of something cruel. Cruelty is an important part of farce and Shakespeare is not afraid to use it. It stops his play becoming sentimental. But, again, you should notice how he blends strong feelings and absurd situations. This is a complex and delightful mixture and it characterizes the whole play.

ACT I SCENE v

This long scene is one of the greatest importance. That blend of emotion and absurdity that we noticed before is particularly rich in this scene.

We have already met two wholly comic characters. Now we meet Feste, the clown. It was the custom of great houses to employ jesters, but Feste is no slapstick figure of fun. Sir Toby and, even more, Sir Andrew Aguecheek, take that role. Feste is an extraordinary mixture. He plays so constantly with words that they seem to lose all fixed meaning. (You *must* refer to the notes in the New Penguin Shakespeare to make sure you really understand his jokes.) He is clearly fond of Olivia, but he is certainly not a lover. He can be very vicious. He can also sing. Sometimes his songs are no more than Sir Toby's tavern ballads, but at other times they are truly beautiful and lead us to see how music can indeed be 'the food of love'. You should see how diverse a figure Feste is. Most of the play's various moods can be found in him: love, poetry, farce, low life, cruelty and revenge. The jester's costume of the period was an odd thing patched together from different colours. So is Feste. He is a patchwork of all the play's moods.

When we first meet Feste he is returning to Olivia's house. No one knows where he has been, though it may be possible to think he was at Orsino's and that perhaps it was he who played the music to the Duke in the first scene. Immediately we see him we hear him playing with words. He is a better wit than Maria. He is also shrewd. He knows that Sir Toby is in love with her and she is quick to shut him up when he tells her so (l.27).

With the arrival of Olivia, Feste gives a virtuoso performance of wit. His words tumble over each other in wonderful confusion and we can see that what he is partly doing is trying to win her favour. He has been absent without leave and his mistress might be angry with him. She is also in mourning for her brother and Feste tries to cheer her. Although he seems well intentioned, there is nothing soft in his approach (ll.65–7). He goes right to the point and this bluntness wins Olivia's attention.

It is when Olivia turns to Malvolio that we are introduced to one of the great, unwittingly comic characters in the play. We can translate his name as 'I mean ill-will' and this is precisely what Malvolio intends. His contemptuous and humourless character will have been obvious from the moment he appeared, but once he starts talking it is apparent that his manner is both sour and dismissive. His deadly hatred of Feste is obvious. Quite simply, he thinks Feste is no good at his job. He says that people do not laugh at him, and a fool has no purpose in life if he cannot make people laugh. Malvolio's is a devastating attack. Notice how Feste says nothing: he does not respond to Malvolio. He is waiting to spring a far more vicious revenge. It is left to Olivia to tell us that Malvolio is 'sick of self-love', that he is so wrapped up in his own self-importance that he has lost his sense of humour. Olivia is right; but in losing his sense of humour, Malvolio has lost his sense of reality. He has also just made sure that through his pride he is heading for a humiliating fall.

Maria then announces that a 'young gentleman' has come to see Olivia. This is, as we know, Viola dressed as Cesario. Maria and Malvolio are sent off to dismiss him, but Sir Toby Belch, wonderfully and comically drunk, comes in to report the news of the arrival. He staggers off again with Feste in attendance. The connection between these two becomes more established.

Malvolio has been unsuccessful in his attempts to dismiss the 'young gentleman', who is most obstinate. He has insisted on seeing Olivia. We know that success is crucial to Viola. By a cruel paradox, she must succeed where others have failed, for, if she manages to woo Olivia, she will stand higher in Orsino's esteem. To Malvolio, Cesario is no more than a contemptible boy, handsome but sharp tongued. Perhaps Olivia has been intrigued by his persistence. She agrees, rather wearily, to hear Orsino's 'embassy'. This, she thinks, will be no more than a tiresome chore.

We have commented on the element of acting in Viola's mission. Orsino himself was fully aware of it. There *is* something slightly absurd about it. The position is made more ridiculous when Viola is unsure to which lady she is supposed to declare Orsino's undying passion. This causes her some embarrassment and Olivia and the audience some laughter. Note that Olivia starts in an ironic mood. She will end the scene quite differently.

Viola answers Olivia back fairly bluntly and forthrightly. She knows she is in a ludicrous position but she is not going to allow herself to be ridiculed. Indeed, Olivia finds her rude, and Viola recognizes that she has been so. She is far from cringingly apologetic, however, and this increases Olivia's interest. What Olivia thought was going to be a tedious chore has turned out otherwise. Her interest has been stimulated. She sends her attendants away. On stage, a good actress will show that this awakening of interest is also an awakening of love. The irony deepens. When Viola is finally allowed to proclaim Orsino's love, Olivia listens because what she hears is a declaration of passion from someone she has suddenly fallen in love with herself. She does not know that Cesario is a woman. She is unaware of the farce. But as you read on, notice how farce mingles with some of the most beautiful love poetry Shakespeare ever wrote (ll.257–65).

When they are left alone, the sudden quickening of Olivia's interest in Cesario makes Orsino's pretence of love seem particularly flat and ridiculous. Olivia is asked to show her face, and, as she lifts her veil, Viola is genuinely moved by her beauty. Suddenly she understands why Orsino thinks he is so much in love. Viola responds by calling Olivia hard hearted and proud, and then declares Orsino's love for her in an even more poetic fashion. As we hear of his 'groans that thunder love' and his 'sighs of fire', we are taken back to the world of extreme romance in which the play opened.

Olivia remains unmoved and the point she makes is a shrewd one. She knows that Orsino has much to recommend him. He is virtuous, noble, rich and honorable. He is also learned, brave and handsome (ll.246–52). He has, in other words, all the desirable attributes a lover should have: 'yet I cannot love him'. Put bluntly, she is not attracted to him. For all the world of romance in which Orsino lives, he does nothing to kindle Olivia's imagination. Viola cannot understand this (ll.253–56). So generous is her own love for Orsino that the pain he suffers moves her, although it is the pain of love for another woman.

That Orsino's love, once moved, should not be returned, is incomprehensible to her.

Olivia asks Cesario what he would do in Orsino's place. Viola answers with one of the most beautiful passages in Shakespeare: the 'willow cabin' speech (ll.257–65). Here at its fullest and most poetic extreme is all the ardour and loyalty of thwarted love, absurd if we take it literally, but deeply moving if we let our imagination run with the words. A special irony is that Viola says what Olivia wants to hear. Viola, dressed as Cesario, has been sent to court Olivia. Now she has been asked what she would do if she herself were Orsino. For Olivia the speech that follows seems to come from Cesario himself and her love is kindled not for Orsino but for his messenger, a girl who happens to be dressed as a boy. Poetry, passion and farce combine. As love is awakened in Olivia, so she comes out of mourning. Orsino had said that when her love for her dead brother turned to love for a living man it would be rich and powerful. So it is.

Left alone, Olivia realizes what has happened to her. She is confused, but also happy. In her desperation to see Cesario again she calls Malvolio and, pulling a ring from her finger, gives it to him and tells him to run after 'that same peevish messenger'. She tells him that Cesario left the ring behind. Malvolio is to return it and tell the 'boy' that Olivia will explain why she cannot love Orsino if he will return the following day. Act I ends with a woman in mourning, who previously shunned company, now welcoming love in a most enthusiastic manner. The situation is both absurd and glowingly passionate.

ACT II SCENE i

The opening of the second Act introduces us to a new character: Sebastian, who is not only Viola's brother, but her twin. Naturally, this will cause more confusion, but it will also be essential in resolving the plot.

Like the shipwrecked Viola, Sebastian mourns his sibling. He surrounds himself with an air of doom and mystery (ll.3–7). He tries to free himself from his companion, Antonio, in order to travel on alone. He is sure that Viola is dead. In his sorrow he tells of her beauty (ll.22–8).

The friendship between Antonio and Sebastian is deep and affectionate. Antonio begs to be allowed to follow Sebastian and be his servant, but the young man declines his company. He is bound for Orsino's court and he will go there alone. Finally, he departs. However, Antonio holds Sebastian in such high regard that he resolves to follow him despite the 'many enemies' he has in Orsino's court. Braving all for the love of his friend, he dashes off after him.

ACT II SCENE ii

Viola is also on her way to Orsino's court. Her interview with Olivia has just finished and she is now overtaken by Malvolio, bearing the ring. Malvolio explains that Olivia is returning the ring and repeats Olivia's assurance that she will have nothing to do with Orsino. Cesario is only to return if he reports Orsino's taking of the ring.

Viola shows good manners by covering Olivia's indiscretions. 'She took the ring of me,' she says to protect her, 'I'll none of it.' The haughty Malvolio throws it on the ground before her, telling her to stoop and pick it up if she thinks it worth her while (ll.13–16). His errand done, he leaves.

Viola is left alone. In her soliloquy (ll.17–41) she not only sums up for the audience the farcical complexities of the plot, but shows, touchingly, her own confusion at the direction events have taken. On stage, the opening of this speech is delightfully comic, but two lines (ll.27–8) are an essential quotation:

> *Disguise, I see thou art a wickedness*
> *Wherein the pregnant enemy does much.*

How true this is, the rest of the play will reveal. We sense once again the desperation in Viola's love for Orsino; 'O time, thou must untangle this, not I' (l.40) is her reflection that she is really powerless to solve her dilemma.

ACT II SCENE iii

The third, delightfully comic, scene takes place at night. It opens with Sir Toby and Sir Andrew Aguecheek, both of whom, we may assume, are slightly drunk. After some banter about being up late, they call for Maria to bring 'a stoup of wine'.

Feste enters to join in the roistering. He is clearly familiar with this and popular with the two knights. Ironically, Sir Andrew rather envies the fool for his skills and has sent him money to reward him for the previous night's entertainment. More money is passed and Feste is persuaded to sing again (l.30). He performs a delightfully poetic and moving love song. Again, the combination of foolery and refined feeling that characterizes the play is clear. Sir Andrew and Sir Toby, perhaps helped by the drink, react somewhat sentimentally to the song and it is Sir Toby who revives their vigour – as is appropriate he should – by suggesting that they 'rouse the night-owl in a catch'. Their wit is indeed roused, and after a brief exchange, they sing their round. This soon gets out of hand and Maria appears to try and quieten them down. Her sharp-tongued common sense adds to the comedy of the drunken men, but only makes Sir Toby even rowdier. The relationship between the drunken knight and the lively, commonsensical serving-maid establishes itself more strongly. It is a human, more basic and under-standable sort of love and it throws the romantic ardour of the others into sharp relief.

Their rowdiness leads to one of the great comic moments in the play: the arrival of Malvolio in his nightgown (l.85). An absurd figure, his costume makes him more absurd still. His pomposity and 'self-love' have already caused us to dislike him. His puritanical and self-righteous disapproval of the others' fun makes him more distasteful.

We begin to enjoy Sir Toby's defiance. At first he merely continues singing, but when Malvolio refuses to go away, the knight turns on him. He pulls rank. Malvolio is not of his class. He is only a commoner. His refusal to enjoy the fun of life and his hypocritical smugness result in a famous put-down: 'Dost thou think, because thou art virtuous, there shall be no more cakes and ale?' (ll.111–12). Feste, too, is furious, and after a bitter parting line, 'Yes, by Saint Anne, and ginger shall be hot i' the mouth, too', he exits.

Weakly, Malvolio threatens to tell Olivia of Maria's behaviour and himself leaves. He has managed to offend all of them: Sir Toby, Feste, Maria, and, simply because he is there, Sir Andrew Aguecheek. They begin to think seriously of revenge.

Sir Andrew, whom we know to be of a quarrelsome nature, suggests challenging Malvolio to a duel (l.123). Sir Toby seconds him. Maria, ever the most sensible, calms them down. Their idea is absurd: a duel is a serious matter and would seriously threaten Olivia's household. She, as Maria reminds us, has been 'much out of quiet' since Viola's visit. Besides, Maria has a much better plan. She knows that Malvolio is a time-serving Puritan, pompous and self-satisfied. He thinks 'all that look on him love him'. Indeed, Malvolio is so caught up in his own vanity that Maria will be able to use it to work his downfall. She says she will pen some rather vaguely phrased love letters to Malvolio, purportedly from Olivia. For Maria and her mistress have very similar handwriting and, from certain remarks in the letter, Malvolio will be able to recognize himself and so believe that Olivia is in love with him (ll.148–54). Nothing could be more unlikely, but so blinded is Malvolio by vanity that he will believe the impossible. This outburst of natural high spirits draws us ever closer to Maria. It has the same effect on Sir Toby. But not for him the refined poetry of love. His description of Maria is much more homely: 'She's a beagle true bred, and one that adores me . . .' (l.172).

The scene ends with Sir Andrew confessing he has spent too much money on his courtship of Olivia (l.177). Sir Toby, nonetheless, bids him send for more. As it is too late to go to bed, the two knights go off to warm and spice some sherry.

ACT II SCENE iv

We return to the world of courtly high romance. Orsino's cry, 'Give me some music' (l.1), recalls the mood of the previous evening: 'If music be the food of love, play on' (I,i,1). We discover that it is Feste the jester who had played it to him. While he is sent for – note again how easily Feste moves between the courts of Olivia and Orsino – the Duke talks to Viola. She, of course, is still disguised as Cesario.

Naturally, the conversation dwells on love. Orsino presents himself as the model of the true lover: constant to the image of his mistress but 'unstaid and skittish in all motions else' (l.18). The irony is that he is talking about the woman he loves, but who does not love him, to another woman in disguise who loves him passionately. Viola's feelings come across to us as she describes the effect of the music (ll.21–2). From this reply, Orsino realizes that Cesario is in love. He bids his page speak of his passion, and Viola is put in the painful position of having to tell the truth without disclosing her identity. She tells Orsino that her lover is about Orsino's age and similar in looks (ll.26–8). Orsino does not realize that she actually means him. How could he? His replies, however, suggests that he is indeed the perfect match for Viola. There is much tender irony in the poetry.

Feste enters to sing his song. Orsino describes it in a way that makes us impatient to hear its beauty, and we are, indeed, rewarded. 'Come away, come away, death' is the most emotive of songs, full of a refined and melancholy sense of death. Feste, sometimes bitter, sometimes boisterous, has the power to move an audience very deeply. To prevent this scene becoming sentimental, Feste leaves the stage on a witty note (ll.72–7).

Viola and Orsino are left alone and once more the Duke requests her to speak to Olivia on his behalf about marriage. Viola gently hints that for all its idealism, Orsino's love is hopeless (l.86). She then reverses the position. Supposing, she says, a woman loved Orsino as much as he loves Olivia. If he could not love her, should she not be told? Orsino's reply is interesting. No woman, he says, could love as strongly as he; a woman's heart is not big enough. The love of women, he says, is a somewhat fickle thing (ll.92–102). His love – a man's love – is 'as hungry as the sea'. There is no comparison between the two. This is male ardour at its most extreme. Time will show what Orsino says to be untrue. His affections will turn to Viola when he finds out that she is indeed a woman and the most constant of lovers.

Viola replies to this on behalf of women. Women *are* as faithful and strong as 'we' men. She knows this through what she is suffering herself. To illustrate her point, she tells Orsino a story which hints at her own passion (ll.106–14). It is a story full of pathos and refined feeling about a maiden who hid her love – as Viola is forced to do – and who died of love so suppressed. Men, Viola says, show more than they actually feel. Woman love strongly and quietly. Men brag but are inconstant.

Orsino asks if Viola's 'sister' died of her love (l.118). Her reply is vague, ambiguous. We are momentarily reminded of her love for Sebastian and then, with a rush of common sense, Viola asks if she should return to Olivia. Orsino bids her go.

ACT II SCENE v

Act II Scene v is a long, delicious farce. It shows Malvolio being completely taken in by Maria's trick.

At the beginning of the scene we are introduced to a new character: Fabian. He is of no great significance to the plot of the play; rather, he acts as the 'straight man' and so helps to make the ensuing scenes more amusing. Fabian, too, bears his own grudge against Malvolio (ll.7–8).

Maria enters, bustling with excitement. She asks the others to hide as Malvolio is approaching. He has, she says, been acting out roles to himself for the past half hour and observing his looks and bearing from his shadow. She puts the letter where she knows he will find it and then runs off. She herself does not watch the ensuing events.

Malvolio enters, declaring how convinced he is that Maria once loved him. The effect is utterly ridiculous. Malvolio appears at once pompous and blind to his faults. What he says, however, makes Sir Toby furious, and much of the fun and comic suspense in the scene come from the fact that while we see them watching Malvolio, he cannot see them. However, they make so much noise that they run the risk of being discovered at any moment. When this scene is produced in a lively way, the effect is most exciting. It has the effect of true farce.

Malvolio's musings change from love to social status (l.34). He begins to imagine himself as 'Count Malvolio', the husband of Olivia. He imagines his new-found grandeur and wealth. He imagines how he will revenge himself on Sir Toby once he is his superior. Malvolio lovingly details each stage of the humiliation (ll.58–77). The fact that Sir Toby is actually watching and hearing adds to the comedy. Malvolio prances about, enjoying his fantasy, and then comes upon Maria's letter. He picks it up and it seems to him almost at once that his fantasies of marriage to Olivia are about to be fulfilled. The bawdy jokes make Malvolio appear yet more vulgar and absurd, but as he begins to interpret the riddles, solving each one so that it seems to prove his point, we see him falling ever more surely into Maria's trap. Every phrase seems to add to Malvolio's assurance: rhymes, the relation of servant to master, all seem to apply to him. Finally, when he is all but convinced that Olivia is secretly in love with him, there follows a passage in prose (ll.139–53). Malvolio is told to 'revolve', in other words 'think' about what he has been reading. Many actors at this point actually turn round, thereby making Malvolio look even more ridiculous. He is told that some people 'have greatness thrust upon 'em'. He should cast off his 'humble slough'. This is what a snake does when it sheds its skin, and the comparison of Malvolio with a snake is intended. He is told to be rude, surly and pompous. Above all – and for the most comic effect – he is told to wear cross-gartered, yellow stockings (ll.148–9).

Malvolio is delighted. With almost pathetic energy and hope he vows to do everything the letter says – in other words make himself look totally ridiculous. For him each suggestion in the letter is a proof of Olivia's love. He has been completely tricked. He will even take up the suggestion in the postscript that he start to smile (l.168). The grimace on the actor's face should reduce us to laughter. After this Malvolio struts off.

Fabian and the two knights are delighted. Sir Toby is so pleased with Maria that he 'could marry this wench for this device'. Indeed, he does. When she comes in we see how much closer together this prank has brought them. Maria is delighted with her success. They all go off to see Malvolio make a complete fool of himself before Olivia.

ACT III SCENE i

The third Act opens with Viola, still disguised as Cesario, making her way to Olivia's court. Before meeting with the lady herself, she encounters first Feste and then Sir Andrew and Sir Toby Belch. Both of these short meetings show her wit.

The meeting with Feste is not without a touch of cynicism and even bitterness, though Feste's main intention is to beg money from her. She then meets with Sir Toby and Sir Andrew, principally that Olivia may send them and Maria away, thereby heightening the sense of intimacy as she and Viola are left alone in the garden with the door shut.

Olivia learns Cesario's name and Viola tries to press on with Orsino's suit. Olivia will have none of it: 'I bade you never speak again of him' (l.104). What she wants is far more difficult and embarrassing than listening to whatever the Duke may wish to say through his messenger. Olivia has, as we know, fallen in love with this messenger. What she wants to hear is a declaration of love from Cesario himself. The position is absurd. It is also, for two reasons, deeply painful. First, the experience of love is not a sweet and simple delight. True passion hurts, and Olivia's is no exception to the rule. Secondly, Olivia has compromised herself and she is well aware of this. She lied to Malvolio about the ring she sent to Cesario and she realizes that Cesario must have guessed her intentions. She is half way to declaring her love for a servant. Her 'honour', as she says — in other words her reputation and her social standing – is at stake. She wonders if Cesario thinks the worst of her. Has she made herself a laughing-stock or is she despised? The worry that underlines such a farcical situation becomes stronger and stronger as the scene progresses and we should watch how Viola – who is perfectly well aware of what is going on and yet cannot, for the moment, reveal who she is – treats the whole matter with great delicacy. She says first that she pities Olivia, and we may believe this (l.120). Olivia, for her part, sees this as a hopeful sign of love. When she is told that it is not so she tries to put a brave face on the matter and to dismiss Cesario with all the dignity she can muster. Viola takes her opportunity to leave but asks Olivia to say nothing of their meeting to Orsino (l.133).

But Olivia's love is stronger than she realizes. She cannot simply let Cesario go. She calls him back and, as she asks 'I prithee, tell me what thou think'st of me?', we begin to be moved by the emotion she so clearly feels. Viola replies (l.136) with a sentence that can mean either: 'You think you are not in love with a woman, but you are'; or, 'In loving a page you are behaving as if you were not born a lady.' Olivia replies that surely Cesario is not what he seems to be. Olivia thinks he is not a pageboy, but a young aristocrat. The confusion here is very delicate and both women are right to think that things are not what they seem. However, in the attempt to free herself from Olivia's unwanted company, it seems that Viola becomes a little angry. The look of beauty and anger in her face is deeply attractive to Olivia, who now bravely – and exquisitely – confesses her love (ll.146–53). Here is a form of love at once painful, hopeless, and, to the audience, deeply moving. Viola herself is moved and tries to persuade Olivia that no woman will ever have her heart. With that, Viola bids farewell and goes. She herself, she says, is the only person who will ever be mistress of her heart. She declares that she will never return and the scene ends with Olivia's desperate plea that she should come back if only to try and persuade her to love Orsino.

This first scene of Act III is a complex one. The farcical situation of a woman in love with another dressed as a boy never really makes us laugh, although we are aware of its potential comedy. Rather, the confused emotions of Olivia and the dignified and poetic way in which she expresses them are both touching and painful. The situation she finds herself in is as cruel as it is comic. The element of pain and even of humiliation that is so important to *Twelfth Night* is here seen very clearly. The play *is* a comedy, but it does not always make us laugh.

ACT III SCENE ii

We return to Sir Toby, Sir Andrew and Fabian. Sir Andrew has managed to glimpse something of the meeting between Olivia and Cesario in the 'orchard', and he is now resolved that he will leave Illyria. He has begun to see the truth: there is no hope whatsoever in his quest for Olivia's hand. She showed 'more favours to the Count's servingman than ever she bestowed upon me' (ll.4–6).

Sir Toby is quick to deny this, for he cannot afford to lose Sir Andrew. Fabian tells Sir Andrew that, far from rejecting him, Olivia has behaved in this way 'only to exasperate you, to awake your dormouse valour' (l.18). Sir Andrew should have taken the initiative, displayed his wit and then 'banged the youth into dumbness'. That would have shown Olivia he is indeed a man. Sir Andrew must now redeem himself, and Sir Toby suggests that he challenge Cesario to a duel: the feeble knight against a woman in the guise of a pageboy. It is a situation rich in comic possibilities and Shakespeare will be quick to exploit them. Sir Andrew is sent off to write his challenge 'in a martial hand' and Sir Toby and Fabian agree to meet him when he has written it. For the moment, Fabian thinks that Sir Toby is only joking in his suggestion of a duel; but he is quite serious. Sir Toby realizes the absurdity of the whole affair and he is going to enjoy every moment of it.

At this point, Maria enters. Sir Toby has just set one ridiculous action in motion, and Maria now comes in to tell them how a second is progressing. Malvolio is about to appear in cross-gartered yellow stockings. He has obeyed 'every point of the letter' and is smiling and strutting his way to his comic downfall. The audience is led to expect two deliciously farcical scenes: Malvolio's courting of Olivia and Sir Andrew Aguecheek's duel with Viola (Cesario).

ACT III SCENE iii

Before these two great scenes of farce, Shakespeare reintroduces us to Sebastian and Antonio. This is important, for not only does it provide a break in the action, a moment of relative dignity, but it is also necessary for establishing the mechanism whereby the plot will be resolved. Antonio has to give Sebastian his purse. Sebastian himself has to be established as walking about near to the scene of the action.

Sebastian thanks Antonio for staying with him and suggests they wander the town (ll.21–4). Antonio cannot accompany him, for he has many enemies there. He has fought in a naval encounter against Orsino and is well known as an enemy of the Count. The motive for his arrest is thus established and, as he gives Sebastian his purse, we are assured not only of the friendship between the two men, but that the purse will be used later in the unfolding of the plot.

ACT III SCENE iv

Act III Scene iv brings the build-up of two comic incidents to a head: the appearance of Malvolio, suitably dressed, and Sir Andrew Aguecheek's duel with Viola. It is all hilariously funny. It also sets in motion the events that will lead to the climax of the play. But, as always in *Twelfth Night*, pure comedy is not Shakespeare's only intention. Olivia's suffering continues the theme of melancholy which is so marked an aspect of the play.

Indeed, the scene starts with Olivia. Her infatuation with Cesario is so strong that she has sent a servant off in pursuit of him. The servant will return (l.57) to announce that he has persuaded Cesario to come back. Olivia, in the meantime, is impatient to see him and her expectancy gives a special absurdity to the sudden appearance of Malvolio. Olivia is waiting for the youth she loves; she will be confronted by her steward – a man wholly unlovable – in the role of a lover.

Olivia's language makes obvious her excitement. Shrewdly, she guesses that Cesario's love may be more easily bought than won. He is young and, she suspects, easily influenced. She is both tense and unhappy and she nervously calls twice for Malvolio, for she hopes his 'sad and civil' nature will match her own feelings. Maria announces his arrival. We side with her and enjoy the fact that she is preparing the scene, but the suggestion of madness in Malvolio is important and will be developed – with considerable cruelty – later on. To Olivia's surprise, Maria tells her that Malvolio 'does nothing but smile' (l.11). This is hardly in keeping with her own mood.

We should perhaps imagine Malvolio as the sort of haughty and sour-faced prig whose face would crack if he smiled. A lover's smile should be generous and confident. Malvolio's is nothing more than absurd. Given that Olivia is waiting for Cesario – the 'man' she really loves – Malvolio's protestations of love seem particularly inappropriate, even vulgar. We laugh at him and we begin to relish the way he unwittingly humiliates himself.

Malvolio declares that his cross-gartering is so tight that he wonders if his circulation is being obstructed (ll.19–20). However, he puts on a brave face and so appears even more insane. The idea of lunacy has already been suggested to us and Malvolio's behaviour is, of course, a parody of the irrational, poetic love of Orsino for Olivia and of Olivia for Cesario. He is acting in the belief that the letter which promised him Olivia's love actually came from her, and he quotes it in defence of Olivia's ever more frantic questioning. He kisses her hand and woos her earnestly. He could appear almost threatening were it not for the fact that it is all so comic. When the comic tension is at its height, the servant enters to announce that Cesario has been persuaded, albeit reluctantly, to return to Olivia. Olivia has been confronted by a comic threat in Malvolio; now she is truly apprehensive about the appearance of the 'man' she loves. She quickly gives orders that Malvolio be 'looked to'. She cares greatly for his welfare for she is sure he is mad. She then goes off, in a state of high excitement, to meet Cesario.

Malvolio, left alone, has a comic soliloquy (ll.65–83). He has heard that Sir Toby will look after him and immediately interprets this as an opportunity to snub him, just as the letter suggested. He preens himself and appears ever more ridiculous. As far as Malvolio is concerned, there is no doubt whatsoever that Olivia is truly in love with him. Remembering that he is a Puritan, Malvolio is careful to thank 'Jove' twice for his good fortune.

Malvolio tries to rebuff Sir Toby when he enters. Sir Toby insists that Malvolio is mad and Fabian and Maria support him. Malvolio's behaviour is certainly absurd. We know, however, that he is not actually insane. Madness is wished onto him by Sir Toby, Fabian and Maria. It is a part of their revenge. We may find it cruel, but cruelty, as we have seen, is rarely far below the surface in *Twelfth Night*. It is an essential part of Shakespeare's comic view of the world. But it would take the element of cruelty too far for us to see Malvolio forcibly led off by the others. His departure is loftily defiant. However, the others relish the degree to which Malvolio has fallen for their ruse and threaten to 'make him mad indeed'. (We should at this point appreciate the difference between the Elizabethan and our contemporary attitude towards insanity. Where we should hope to have a compassionate understanding, Elizabethans treated the mad both cruelly and as a source of amusement.) We see here Sir Toby vowing to take Malvolio to a 'dark room' and tie him down and bate him (l.134). For Sir Toby, vigorous and worldly, this will be both a 'pastime' and a 'pleasure'. It will also be a triumph of comic revenge.

Sir Andrew now enters and reads out part of his absurd challenge to Cesario. His hot temper is ridiculous and the others realize this. Sir Toby, Fabian and Maria find him amusing, as does the audience. Maria tells Sir Andrew that Cesario is even now with Olivia, and Sir Toby urges on him the utmost masculine bravado. Sir Andrew rushes off, consumed with his absurd desire for the duel.

Sir Toby realizes that Sir Andrew's challenge, with its flat, ridiculous sentences, will appear as ridiculous to Cesario as to everyone else.

He also understands that to get the greatest fun out of the duel he must deliver Sir Andrew's challenge by word of mouth, painting in the knight's absence a terrifying picture of Sir Andrew's 'rage, skill, fury, and impetuosity'. Sir Toby and Fabian stand aside, Sir Toby to 'meditate the while upon some horrid message for a challenge' (ll.195–6).

Viola and Olivia enter. We move now from farce to high emotion. The interview between them is short but poignant. Olivia knows her love is being rejected (ll.197–8) and she is sorry she has expressed herself as she has. Viola, for her part, repeats again Orsino's love for Olivia. Olivia presses her own love but Viola deflects it, offering to release Olivia from her promises so that she may offer her love to Orsino (l.211). With that she leaves, but Olivia's depth of suffering is clearly expressed: 'A fiend like thee might bear my soul to hell' (l.213).

It is as Viola leaves that we see Shakespeare's real reason for bringing her back on stage. Her appearance has not only reinforced the idea of Olivia's love, but it also brings her to her meeting with Sir Toby and Fabian who deliver a challenge from Sir Andrew Aguecheek. Viola is quite severely threatened here, as she thinks. Sir Toby is a master of creating illusions, and his description of Sir Andrew Aguecheek's furious valour is at once intimidating to Viola and comic to us. We know how absurd it is; she does not. Indeed, she tries to avoid the duel, but to no effect. Sir Toby will have his fun and he insists that Sir Andrew must be met. Again, the blend of comedy and pathos is strong. We admire Viola for her behaviour and we do not like to see her so threatened. On the other hand, the prospect of the duel between a woman dressed as a man and a man who is a cowardly fop promises to be amusing.

And so it proves, for Sir Toby is a master of effects. Having frightened Viola into showing her wholly understandable reluctance to fight, Sir Toby then proceeds to scare Sir Andrew by lying enormously about Cesario's valour. A duel – which should be a vigorous and fearsome matter – is here to be fought out by two frail cowards.

As Viola enters, Sir Toby takes pleasure in building up the fear of both parties. Viola's suffering is quite genuine, and we feel for her even in our enjoyment. Sir Andrew's cowardice is merely absurd. Nonetheless, both adversaries feel obliged to begin the sham duel to prove that they are men. They draw their swords.

Antonio enters at once. It is something no one could have predicted. Of course, he mistakes Viola for Sebastian. They are almost identical twins and Viola's masculine disguise removes the most obvious signs of difference. This moment offers some relief. A real man has come to Viola's aid. It is a moment of almost pure farce. A more contrived coincidence than Antonio's arrival and a more absurd misunderstanding than his mistaking her for Sebastian could not easily be imagined. In the theatre, this scene usually meets with a great deal of amusement.

But the audience laughs only for a moment. The Officers come in and arrest Antonio there and then. All three, Viola, Sir Andrew and Antonio, are caught with their swords drawn. Sir Andrew quickly makes his peace, but the Officers arrest Antonio. He is a known enemy of Orsino's and the First Officer recognizes him: 'I know your favour well,/Though now you have no sea-cap on your head' (ll.320–21). It is all absurd, unlikely and very, very funny.

Antonio realizes that he has no alternative but to go with the Officers and he turns to Viola whom he still thinks is Sebastian. He asks for the return of the purse he gave him and his request is both comic and touching. Viola, naturally, is dumbfounded. She cannot imagine what her rescuer, now arrested, can possibly mean. She has neither met him before nor borrowed money from him. She is, of course, affected by the position Antonio finds himself in and she offers to lend him half of what little money she has (l.335). Antonio rounds on her, still thinking she is Sebastian, amazed at what he can only consider to be ingratitude. He is outraged as he explains how he saved the young man, whom he thinks is standing before him, from the sea. The Officers lead him away convinced that he, like so many other characters in the play, is 'mad'. Antonio is naturally very bitter; once again, as so often in the play, bitterness mingles with farce.

For Viola, however, there is hope. Antonio has mentioned her brother Sebastian by name. The fact that she must have been mistaken for her brother suggests that he is probably still alive. As Sir Toby,

Fabian and Sir Andrew Aguecheek talk, her love for her brother rises to the rapturous expression of the hope that he may still be living.

The other three are left on stage, Sir Andrew protesting his valour, and Fabian keen to see how things will turn out.

ACT IV SCENE i

Feste has been sent to beg Viola, still disguised as Cesario, to return once again to Olivia. His words open the fourth Act, but it is not to Viola he is speaking. He has encountered Sebastian, Viola's twin brother, and he has totally confused this young man for the Cesario of the earlier Acts.

The misunderstanding leads to comedy. Sebastian answers Feste back with none of Cesario's typical bashfulness. By so doing, he brings out Feste's satirical wit. However, Sebastian soon buys him off.

Their conversation is short, but it is important. It prepares us for the increasingly ludicrous confusion that Sebastian – Cesario's apparently identical twin – will cause as the Act progresses. Indeed, no sooner has Sebastian left Feste than Sir Andrew comes in, accompanied by Fabian and Sir Toby. At the end of the last Act, Sir Andrew Aguecheek vowed to chase after Cesario and 'beat him'. Now he mistakes Sebastian for Cesario and strikes him. Sebastian, utterly bewildered, strikes him back. He has just had an incomprehensible conversation with Feste; now he has been struck by a total stranger. We laugh as we hear him ask if all the people in Illyria are mad. It seems as if they are.

Feste slips out to inform Olivia of what is going on. Sir Toby, meanwhile, his temper raised by Sir Andrew's humiliation, urges him to fight back. Sir Andrew, an inveterate coward, will have none of it. He would rather see the young man in court than fight him. Sir Toby grabs Sebastian and tries to arrest him, presumably on the grounds that Sebastian has caused a breach of the peace and struck a knight. Sebastian, in anger, draws his sword. Sir Toby, in turn, draws his.

Olivia enters at once. She thinks that Sir Toby is about to fight with her beloved Cesario. She tells Sir Toby in no uncertain terms to depart, calling him a 'rudesby', a ruffian. Sir Toby obeys her and Olivia is left alone with the young man whom she thinks is Cesario. When reading the play it is important to remember at this point not only that Olivia is very beautiful, but that Sebastian had never set eyes on her before. When she shows so much concern for him, concern that can only spring from love, the effect is yet again both moving and comic. At last, it seems to her, Olivia really has a chance to care for Cesario. She shows great concern for him and invites him to her house.

Sebastian is quite dumbfounded by events. First a fool has approached him, then he has been struck and challenged by a roistering knight. Now a beautiful woman – a complete stranger – has invited him to her house with every show of affection. Perhaps he turns to the audience with an aside to express his wonder and confusion (ll.59–62). The audience certainly laughs as Sebastian willingly lets himself be swept up into the world of all but insane love that characterizes Illyria (ll.60–62):

> *Or I am mad, or else this is a dream.*
> *Let fancy still my sense in Lethe steep;*
> *If it be thus to dream, still let me sleep!*

Sebastian departs willingly; we should, in our amusement, consider what we are laughing at: the absurdity of Olivia's extreme and confused romantic passion.

ACT IV SCENE ii

The next scene is more bitter, even cruel. Sebastian has willingly let himself be swept off into the delights of near madness and love. The second scene, however, presents the taunting of a would-be lover – Malvolio – as if he were truly insane. This is the revenge of Feste, Sir Toby and Sir Andrew.

Feste, developing the theme of disguise, dresses up as Sir Topas, the priest. He acts out this part, probably disguising his accent as well as using a different vocabulary. Sir Toby throughly enjoys the illusion.

Malvolio, the restrained lunatic, is locked in his darkened cell. Unable to see what is really going on, he thinks he can hear voices. Pathetically, he calls out to them, desperately and repeatedly, that he is perfectly sane. He may be, but how can he prove it? It is his word against Feste's and Feste bears a grudge against Malvolio. He turns everything Malvolio says into proof of his madness. Malvolio talks of 'nothing but ladies', and when he declares that his cell is dark, Feste replies in a complex way. Every one of his ideas is a logical impossibility: 'bay windows transparent as barricadoes' are opaque, the 'south-north' is an impossible direction, 'lustrous as ebony' is a contradiction in terms.

Malvolio's protestations of sanity become increasingly desperate. Feste begins to test his power to reason. Malvolio rejects utterly the idea that 'the soul of our grandam might haply inhabit a bird' (l.51) but is told that he will remain in darkness even though he can reason like a sane man.

In fact, as Maria points out, Feste did not need to dress himself as Sir Topas: Malvolio could not see him anyway. Feste now goes back to him at Sir Toby's bidding, though we should notice that Sir Toby is far from happy with the whole procedure (ll.68–70). The joke has gone far enough. He fears that Olivia will be upset, for she respects Malvolio as a good servant. She is also angry with Sir Toby for attacking the young man they all think is Cesario. Sir Toby leaves with Maria, hoping that Feste will find a convenient way of releasing Malvolio from his cell.

But Feste still bears his grudge. He sings, without attempting to disguise his voice, outside Malvolio's cell and takes no notice of the steward's desperate pleading. He continues to insist that Malvolio is mad – no better than Feste himself, the known and recognized fool. This, of course, is Feste's personal revenge for Malvolio's slighting of him in Act I Scene v. Feste enjoys his revenge. Invisible to Malvolio, he alternates his own voice with that of Sir Topas, until the desperate

Malvolio bids Feste bring him ink, paper and a light. Malvolio wishes to write to Olivia and says he will reward Feste. This wins the fool over. He goes away, but we should notice how he departs singing a mad song.

The end of the scene is haunting and, finally, quite as cruel as it is funny, a combination we have met before in the play.

ACT IV SCENE iii

Sebastian enters, still full of wonder. His rapture is both genuine and, to the audience, comic. He too is convincing us he is not mad, though he fully and not surprisingly admits to his wonder. He is loved by a beautiful woman he has never seen before. He has been given a pearl. He recognizes that he urgently needs Antonio's advice. Because he cannot believe what has happened to him he needs to talk to someone to prove that he is not mad. We should, of course, notice the parallel here with Malvolio who has also been trying to prove himself sane. Olivia, despite her behaviour, is clearly in her right mind. As Sebastian recognizes, she is an intelligent woman who runs her household smoothly.

Sebastian no sooner mentions Olivia than she comes in, accompanied by a priest. She insists on an immediate and secret betrothal, an engagement. Sebastian willingly agrees. Olivia, naturally, is utterly delighted to think that she has finally won the man with whom she is in love.

ACT V SCENE i

The last Act is one long, superlative scene. It opens with Fabian begging Feste to show him Malvolio's letter, but no sooner has Feste refused this than Orsino and Viola enter.

Orsino and Feste exchange witticisms, Feste making quite sure that he is financially rewarded for his, though he fails to win a third gold coin from the Duke. Orsino orders Feste to tell Olivia he has come to see her. He has come to woo her, of course. If Feste actually manages to bring Olivia back with him, 'it may', says Orsino 'awake my bounty further' (ll.40–41).

As Feste leaves, Antonio enters with the Officers. Viola recognizes him at once as the man who rescued her. Orsino also recognizes him at once as the man who, as the captain of a worthless little boat, fought valiantly against him (ll.48–56). The first Officer exposes Antonio as a pirate and states he arrested him in a public affray. Viola confirms how Antonio helped her but refers to the 'strange speech' he put on her: in other words to the business about the rescue and the purse. Orsino is furious that Antonio should be so rash as to come to Illyria and risk arrest.

Antonio denies that he is a pirate, though he confesses 'on base and ground enough' to being Orsino's enemy. He explains that he has come to Illyria because of the strong love he has for Sebastian, the young and ungrateful man who, as he believes, is standing by Orsino at this moment. He explains how he saved Sebastian's life. For his sake he exposed himself to the dangers of the town and defended him when he was challenged by Sir Andrew Aguecheek. He suggests that Sebastian – as he believes Viola to be – declined to know him out of 'false cunning'. He did not wish to be arrested and so showed the true shallowness of his friendship. Sebastian would not even return his purse. Antonio's bitterness is obvious.

And so is Viola's confusion. Orsino, keen to get to the bottom of the matter, asks when Viola first came to the town. Antonio replies that he and Sebastian arrived that day, having been wandering together for three months.

At this moment Olivia appears. It is the first time in the play that she and Orsino have met. He, for his part, is thrown into sudden rapture. He dismisses Antonio as a madman whose story bears no relationship to the truth and orders him to be taken aside.

Olivia coldly asks what she can do for Orsino beyond love him, which she is unable to do. She also confuses Viola (still dressed as Cesario) with Sebastian. She is very surprised to see him with Orsino, who is, as she thinks, his old master. Both Viola and Orsino try to speak. Olivia again makes it clear that she will not hear declarations of Orsino's love for her. Orsino accuses Olivia of being cruel and perverse. He asks, perhaps somewhat desperately, what he should now do. His elaborate courtship has had no effect on Olivia at all. She tells Orsino to do whatever he likes, provided it 'shall become him'.

Orsino replies in a fury, the vengeance of thwarted love both bitter and vicious. This represents, perhaps, the high point of cruelty and danger in the play. It is a pointed comment on the madness and extremism of romantic passion. Orsino wonders first why he should not kill Olivia. Such 'savage jealousy', he thinks, almost 'savours nobly'. But he knows why he has been rejected. He is aware of Olivia's love for Cesario: 'this your minion, whom I know you love'. He admits that he himself is fond of Cesario and he swears a terrible revenge. He will kill Viola in Olivia's place (ll.123–9). This is Viola's moment of greatest crisis and, as the proof of her love, she cries out (ll.130–31):

> And I, most jocund, apt, and willingly
> To do you rest, a thousand deaths would die.

And she follows Orsino, swearing that she loves him more than her own life.

If this is a moment of high drama, it is also the moment when the combination of farce and grand feeling is most subtly combined. 'Cesario's' declaration of love for Orsino is incomprehensible to Olivia. She still confuses Viola with Sebastian and feels desperately cheated, 'beguiled'. 'Who does beguile you? Who does do you wrong?', Viola demands. Can Cesario really have forgotten, Olivia wonders. After all, only some little while before they plighted their troth. She calls for the priest, and, while he is brought and Orsino begins to lead Viola off with a terse, brutal 'Come, away!', Olivia calls out to the person she thinks is her 'husband'. Olivia's confusion here is both pathetic and very funny. The bewilderment that results from it – Orsino's amazement, Olivia's insistence, Viola's protestations – all come in quick and dramatic succession. Just before the priest enters, Olivia urges Cesario to be brave, to stand by his vow of marriage. She then turns to the priest, who previously she had made swear to 'conceal' all, and now tells him to reveal all. This the priest fulsomely does. Orsino turns on Viola. It seems to him that the youth he sent to woo Olivia for him has won the lady for himself. If such lying and duplicity is the way in which this young man's life has begun, what a villain will he be when he is mature, Orsino declares. Utterly disillusioned, he turns to leave. In his apparently understandable fury he directs Viola to ensure they never meet again. She protests, but her cries are countered by Olivia and the arrival of Sir Andrew Aguecheek claiming that both he and Sir Toby have been badly hurt by 'one Cesario'. For her part, Viola, utterly bewildered, strongly denies the accusations just as the drunken Sir Toby limps in. No doubt his wounds are grossly exaggerated and even funny. The doctor is slow to come and attend him, but Sir Andrew offers his help and Sir Toby, bitterly accepting this, limps out with him, Fabian and Feste. We shall not see Sir Toby Belch again.

Sebastian enters immediately on this, bursting with apology for his attack on Sir Toby. Olivia looks at him in total amazement. Here, just arrived, is the seemingly identical twin of the young man who was standing by Orsino and to whom she thought she was betrothed.

It is to Antonio that Sebastian first turns, greeting him with great affection. Antonio is as confused as everyone. 'Sebastian, are you?', he asks. Sebastian, for his part, wonders how Antonio can doubt it. Antonio points to the 'two creatures' – Sebastian and Viola – in amazement. They are as alike as two halves of an apple.

Having made us laugh at the ridiculous situation, Shakespeare now offers his audience something more subtle. We move, as so often in the play, from farce to high emotion. The exchange between Sebastian and Viola, between newly reunited brother and sister, has an element of the absurd in it quite as strong as the confusion we have just seen. However, it has more: a tenderness and wonder which on stage can be very moving indeed. Each twin had thought the other dead. Neither can now believe his luck. They approach each other tentatively, asking questions, remembering the grief over what they thought was the other's drowning. They question each other over little family details –

moles, the date of their father's death, the sort of intimate details that would indeed prove their relationship to each other. Each even wonders if the other is a ghost. The whole interview comes finally to a joyful and deeply touching climax of reconciliation.

And it is in her joy and her new-found security in knowing that once again she has a protector in her brother that Viola feels able to reveal herself in her true identity. She will now put aside her 'masculine usurped attire' and, when every detail has been confirmed, she will allow Sebastian to embrace her as her brother. She will also tell him how she has served Orsino.

Sebastian turns to Olivia, the woman to whom he is betrothed. He gently but humorously points out her mistake and explains how, through her betrothal to him, she is allied to a man who, as a virgin, can pun on the word 'maid' and so let Olivia see that she is 'betrothed both to a maid and man' (1.260).

Orsino vouches for Sebastian's noble birth and then with a suddenness that is both comic and, for the audience, rather a relief, turns to Viola. Now that he knows her to be a woman and, more, a woman in love with him, he will marry her. She rapturously accepts his love and promises to dress herself in her 'woman's weeds'. The Captain who saved her has these. Then suddenly she remembers. Malvolio has had this man imprisoned. We have had no idea of this up to now and you may have found this incident confusing or even merely ridiculous, a piece of bad plotting on Shakespeare's part. It does not come across as such in the theatre. Many people may not even notice it. The more quickwitted, after all the absurd surprises and revelations in the play, will now accept anything – even this – as part of the fun. The whole situation is so bizarre, so delightfully absurd, that one more blatantly comic gambit is very welcome.

Mention of Malvolio also has a dramatic purpose. In this great last act of resolutions, Malvolio too must be brought onto the stage. His is the last 'madness' to be resolved.

This theme of madness is heightened by the entrance of Fabian and, more important, Feste, who brings Malvolio's letter with him. The fool's hatred for Malvolio is still very strong. After all, he could have given the letter to Olivia much earlier, but, since Malvolio is 'mad' and what he writes must therefore be nonsense, it does not really matter very much when Feste gives the letter to Olivia. In other words, Feste has let Malvolio suffer for as long as he possibly can. When he begins to read the letter he bawls out its contents in the voice of a madman. This clearly annoys Olivia; no doubt the whole trick played on her steward has annoyed her. She is, we should remember, fond of Malvolio for he is a good servant. She asks Fabian to read his letter and perhaps we can imagine her taking it from Feste and giving it to him.

The letter, full of justifiable anger, shows Malvolio to be remarkably sane, as Olivia points out. She orders his immediate release and then turns to Orsino. He should now think of her favourably, not as a wife, but rather as a sister-in-law. She and Sebastian and Orsino and Viola will have a joint wedding for which she will pay (ll.315–16). Orsino readily accepts this. Viola, too, welcomes her new relationship with Olivia.

After this noble and touching reconciliation amongst the aristocrats, Malvolio, the servant, enters. There is pathos in his anger. He has been done a 'notorious wrong', and he is determined the world should know about it. He brandishes Maria's letter at Olivia. Can she deny she wrote it? It is in her handwriting and bears her seal. Why, then, he pathetically asks, has she built up his hopes so only to humiliate him, turning him into 'the most notorious geck and gull/That e'er invention played on?' (ll.341–2).

Olivia looks at the letter. The handwriting is not hers. It is similar to hers, but it is actually Maria's. Then she remembers how it was Maria who first told her Malvolio was mad. She realizes something of what has happened and promises that Malvolio will be allowed to punish the offenders as he chooses. Fabian then steps in to explain what has happened (ll.353–66). He tells us and the company on stage that Sir Toby has married Maria as a reward for her tricks. The audience, of course, is delighted by this. The last we saw of Sir Toby – indeed the last we see of him at all – was him limping off to have his wounds tended. Fabian then asks Olivia – and, by extension, us – to think of the trick played on Malvolio as 'sportful malice', a joke to be dismissed with laughter rather than revenge. After all, as he says, there has been wrong on both sides.

Olivia certainly feels compassion for her steward. Feste, however, reminds us of the bitterness that plays such an important part in *Twelfth Night*. He taunts Malvolio with his shattered hopes of greatness. He tells him that it was he, Feste, who played Sir Topas and cruelly mimicked Malvolio's voice. He then quotes (or rather paraphrases) the words with which Malvolio put him down in Act I Scene v (ll.78–84). 'And thus', Feste adds, 'the whirligig of time brings in his revenges.'

At this, Malvolio storms out, uttering one of the most famous lines in the play: 'I'll be revenged on the whole pack of you!' (l.375). It is a dramatic but sad and even moving moment. We can only hope Fabian will be allowed to 'entreat him to a peace', for the play is, after all, a comedy, and comedies are defined by their happy endings. However, we are not to know if Fabian is successful.

We now come to the happy conclusion reserved for the noble lovers. As is so typical of the play, sadness and joy are juxtaposed. When Viola has met with the Captain who saved her 'and golden time convents', the marriage will take place. Orsino, meantime, will stay at Olivia's house, and he calls Cesario to him: 'For so you shall be, while you are a man', to lead the party off to marriage, harmony and peace.

It is a moment of contentment, even of triumph. The audience is left finally with Feste, the most complex and various of the play's characters. The melancholy beauty of his final song closes the Act and the play itself.

Characters

ORSINO

Orsino opens the play and his first speech is one of the most famous in *Twelfth Night*. It expresses extreme romantic ardour, a way of loving that is poetic, inspired, 'fantastical'. Here we see a man ruled by his emotions, who relishes playing the part of the great lover. He thoroughly enjoys analysing his feelings and indulging his moods (II, iv, 17–20). He is a rare and exquisite creature. He lives in a world of fantasy that is both very beautiful and, ultimately, slightly ridiculous.

We have seen all the way through *Twelfth Night* how poetry and comedy lie side by side. In his behaviour, Orsino is no exception to this. The depths of love that he finds in himself and the language he uses to express them are beautiful beyond doubt. They are also self-indulgent to an almost absurd degree. For with whom is Orsino in love? His ideal woman is Olivia. She is beautiful, certainly, but at the start of the play she is withdrawn, and all the way through she is certain of the simple fact that she does not love Orsino and that she never will. When we accept this, all Orsino's posturing, his belief that Olivia must inevitably be won over, begins to look mildly absurd. Orsino displays himself like a gorgeous peacock, but the object of his affections is not the slightest bit interested.

If we look at the way Shakespeare has constructed the play, Orsino's absurd, impossibly idealized ardour becomes more obvious. Notice that Orsino and Olivia meet only once. The last Act is the single occasion when they confront each other face to face. And what happens? Olivia tells Orsino she is engaged to another man. His grand posturings have had no effect on her at all. Up to this time we have seen Orsino glorying and indulging his emotions on his own. We and his courtiers know he is in love. He has left us in no doubt about that, but his woman has become an ideal, a fantasy in his own mind, hardly a creature of flesh and blood at all. The game of love has become all important to Orsino and this is perhaps most clear when he sends Viola – the woman who really loves him – to do his wooing for him.

As we listen to Orsino talking to his courtiers about his love (Act I Scene i) and then, in a most beautiful scene, discussing its nature with Viola (Act I I I Scene iv) we come to realize that here is a man who has become obsessed with the idea of wooing. We can say that for most of the play Orsino is a study of a man who is in love with love. This is an illusion out of which he has to grow.

Orsino's being in love with love is thus part of the whole idea of illusion and reality in the play (see pp. 76–7). After all, his passion is based on an illusion: the illusion that Olivia will finally be won over. She will not. She has never been anything but honest about this. Orsino, in fact, has become rather a bore to her (I,v,103). So obsessed has he become with the idea of wooing this lady, however, that he has come to live in a world of daydreams, a beautiful world of unreal fantasies. We cannot help being moved by him. We are touched and even amazed by a man so wholly taken over by love. We almost forget how unreal and slightly absurd he is. While Shakespeare is certainly concerned to impress us with Orsino's passion, he is also concerned to show us that it is an illusion – a lie, if we want to use a harsher word – and people cannot live by lies. In *Twelfth Night*, the characters grow out of lies and illusions. They come finally to live in a world of truth and real love. To alert us to how ridiculous lies and illusions are, Shakespeare makes us laugh, or at least smile, at them. We laugh at Malvolio, for instance. How preposterous his courtship of Olivia is. But Orsino is also courting the same lady. To be sure, he does not make himself absurd in yellow stockings and cross-garters. We do not laugh at him outright. Nonetheless, Shakespeare does want us to see that in some ways Orsino's love is like Malvolio's: both are based on illusions. Orsino is in love with a woman who can neither take his love seriously nor respond to it in any way at all. In his extremes, Orsino does indeed make himself look rather foolish.

But in the end his illusions are shattered. Finally, after a long, hopeless courtship and the sending of repeated messengers, he meets Olivia and finds she is engaged. His dream world crumbles around him. How he responds is very important (V,i,115–29). He turns to Viola – who is still disguised as Cesario, the pageboy – and threatens death to the person he believes is his rival. It is a serious moment. When Malvolio's illusions of love are shattered he is branded a madman. He is taken away, much to the audience's amusement. When Orsino's illusions of love are shattered, he momentarily ponders insane violence. He thinks of murder.

It is Viola – disguised as Cesario – whom Orsino wishes to kill. Without realizing it, Orsino wants to murder the one woman who can offer him real love.

Viola has stood by him throughout. She has been unable to reveal herself in her true light, but we have seen the depth and purity of her feelings throughout the play. She loves Orsino purely and completely. He tells her of his passion for Olivia and she is moved because she pities him. He puts her in the most painful and humiliating position when he orders her to go and woo his lady for him. She accepts all this. When she explains the depth of Orsino's love to Olivia we see how very deeply Viola herself is touched by it. She understands how the man she loves so much can, in his turn, be moved by so beautiful a woman. She can describe his passion in great and poignant poetry (I,v,257–65). For him she will suffer all this indignity, all the abuse of Olivia's household. Finally, when Orsino understands that Olivia has fallen in love with her – thinking her to be Cesario, the pageboy – she will even be willing to sacrifice her life for him on the altar of his jealousy. He threatens to murder her and she willingly accepts the prospect of death (V,i,130–31).

Of course, Viola is saved. Sebastian enters and we move suddenly from what could have been tragic – the murder of Viola – to what is very funny and very touching – the reunion of identical twins and the discovery that Viola is not a boy at all. We have laughter and joy, which is how comedy should be. We want a happy ending.

So what of Orsino? It seemed he was about to lose everything: the woman he thought he loved, the pageboy he had trusted and of whom he had grown fond. Then Viola is revealed for the woman she really is: young, beautiful and in love with Orsino. Orsino makes a sudden and complete about face. Since he cannot marry Olivia, he will have this woman instead. We are delighted for Viola's sake. But we laugh too. What did all his ardour for Olivia mean if it can be so lightly cast off? It means precisely what Shakespeare was concerned to show us: that it was an illusion. At a touch from real life it melts away and Orsino can marry the woman who truly loves him. He never courted her, never put on his peacock's performances of passion for her. The woman did the wooing, not the man.

But if Orsino discovers the truth and marries the woman he loves, that does not mean the old, romantic lover has changed at all. Read the last line he utters in the play. He has found his true love and is about to marry her. But see what she has become: 'Orsino's mistress, and his fancy's queen' (1.385). The great romantic of the opening scene is about to leave us. He is still the great romantic, but now he is in love with his future wife rather than a cold, distant lady. His feelings centre around a real woman and the real world. He has been saved from illusion by a woman's love.

VIOLA

> *We men may say more, swear more, but indeed*
> *Our shows are more than will; for still we prove*
> *Much in our vows, but little in our love.*
>
> (II,iv,115–17)

While Orsino is the great romantic who spends most of the play in love with love, Viola is a true lover who spends most of the play disguised as a boy. Only when the illusions of both have been stripped away can these two look forward to the truth: to a shared life of married love.

Viola's words quoted at the beginning of this character study are important. They are spoken while she is dressed as a boy. They express the insights of a woman. What they say, in direct terms, is that men like Orsino make a great show of being in love, but women like herself give themselves quietly, strongly and wholly.

This is the essence of Viola: she is young, beautiful and emotionally strong. When she lands in Illyria she thinks her brother may well be dead. She is deeply upset but she does not, unlike Olivia, abandon herself to unnatural mourning. Under dreadful circumstances (though we must also see that they are comic) she gets on with real life. This is not something at which the native Illyrians are very good. It is something to which Viola will introduce them. Viola shows us true love, and it is through her that characters grow out of their illusions.

Viola is attractive. She is young and lively and she invites our trust. The effect she has on Orsino – despite her being disguised as a boy – is certainly immediate. Within three days he has told her his life story (I,iv,13–14). It is only at the end of this scene that we learn how Viola has fallen deeply in love with Orsino. It is from this love – and from her natural ability to attract love – that everything in the plot springs.

It would be quite wrong for Viola repeatedly and directly to express her love for Orsino. He is the poet and the one who strikes the postures. Perhaps the lines already quoted (p. 54) suggest that Viola knows this. Her love for Orsino shows itself in action not words. But what does she do? Put simply, since she is acting as Orsino's page, she does as she is told: she goes out to try to win Orsino a wife. She is successful in actually getting to see Olivia because she is so forthright. She will brook no opposition from Malvolio and Olivia's interest is aroused by her 'rude' approach. For a while the two women bandy the clichés of courtship (I,v,185–220), but at the close of the scene Viola has risen to the heights of the poetry in her 'willow cabin' speech. What started as being ridiculous and cruelly humiliating – a woman disguised as a boy going to court the woman beloved by the man she herself loves – becomes deeply moving. Viola has shown three things here: her fighting spirit, her capacity for hiding her feelings and her love for Orsino which is composed of complete generosity and selflessness.

Viola's beauty, liveliness and loving nature have another important effect: Olivia is distracted from her unnatural grief and falls headlong in love. Again, the situation is ridiculous: a rather distant woman has fallen hopelessly not only for a serving boy, but the messenger of the man she cannot love and who is, in fact, a woman. As Viola comments (I I,ii,33–6):

> *How will this fadge? My master loves her dearly;*
> *And I, poor monster, fond as much on him;*
> *And she, mistaken, seems to dote on me.*
> *What will become of this?*

The short answer is that things only deteriorate. Her love for Orsino grows by the minute and yet she can only discuss it in a veiled, painful way (I I,iv,106–17). Olivia presses her suit to such extremes that Viola must show all her good manners and evenness of temper. In addition, she is threatened by Sir Toby and Sir Andrew Aguecheek. Thus much she suffers in loving Orsino.

There is more. In the confusion of the last Act, Orsino rightly believes that Viola (dressed as Cesario) has won Olivia's love. Both he and Olivia wrongly believe that the lady is engaged to Cesario. Neither realizes that Olivia is in fact engaged to Viola's twin brother, Sebastian. How does Orsino regard this? It seems to him that the pretty pageboy he trusted so much has run off with the woman he loves. He feels bitterly betrayed and he threatens murder (V,i,115–29):

> *Why should I not – had I the heart to do it –*
> *Like to th'Egyptian thief at point of death*
> *Kill what I love –*
>
> ...
>
> *Come, boy, with me, my thoughts are ripe in mischief.*
> *I'll sacrifice the lamb that I do love*
> *To spite a raven's heart within a dove.*

This is a moment of great danger, for death is threatened here where it was not, for instance, in the duel with Sir Andrew Aguecheek. Orsino, in his rage, wants to kill Viola. This is the supreme test for

Viola: she has suffered and been humiliated, and now her life is being openly threatened. Such is her love for Orsino that she only answers him (V,i,130–31):

> *And I, most jocund, apt, and willingly*
> *To do you rest, a thousand deaths would die.*

She is ready to go with him even to death.

This is a comedy and so, of course, Viola is spared, with a happy ending to the play.

What have we learnt of Viola's character so far? That she is plucky, generous and practical. When she is saved from the shipwreck she realizes that she must get on with life again, despite the likelihood that her brother is dead. She rewards the Captain who saves her and goes off to meet whatever Fate has in store for her. Most important of all, she has the ability to inspire love in other people and to love others in return. Though dressed as a page, she wins Orsino's trust and affection. She woos Olivia away from her unnatural grief and back into the world of warm and living people. She can be strong and forthright. She has a freshness and a lack of artificiality that are very welcome in the rarefied and over-sophisticated atmosphere of Illyria. She does not, as do both Orsino and Olivia, resort to melodramatic extremes. She does not abandon herself to intense grief or hopeless love. She is placed in some very compromising situations, but if she suffers, she does not despair. Because she is healthy and natural, she is resilient.

Above all, Viola has the capacity to love. She loves wholly, generously and selflessly, and it is this that makes her willingly accept whatever Orsino offers: even humiliation and the threat of death. But there is nothing mawkish about Viola as there is about Orsino and Olivia. She alone has constant and deep feelings, knows love and accepts it; she is vibrant, alive and active. She wins our hearts from the start and she never does anything which threatens to lose our affection.

That is why we are glad that the final outcome brings her happiness. Throughout the play – and although in disguise – she has been real and she has been true. What a flood of delicate and honest feeling comes across to us as she is reunited with her brother. How right it is that it should be Viola who wins Olivia and Orsino away from illusions and false love. When Viola can throw off her boy's disguise and reveal herself for who she truly is she can win true love in marriage. She can rouse love and return love. She can lead people from illusion into reality.

OLIVIA

Olivia is the cold, distant woman who has yet to learn the ways of love. All that we know of her at first suggests she has renounced the world to go into mourning for her brother. Valentine returns from his unsuccessful embassy to describe her as a 'cloistress', and the Captain who saves Viola adds that Olivia's father has also died, confirming that she has 'abjured the sight ... of men'. Such extreme reactions are unnatural, an illusion. It is part of Viola's role to dispel them.

Added to this withdrawal from the world is the fact that Olivia is being courted by Orsino whom she simply does not and cannot love. She is never other than straightforward about this. She sends Valentine away, and when she admits Viola – dressed as Cesario – she makes her position clear (I,v,268–71). In Act V Scene i, when she has become engaged to Sebastian, her answer is still the same (l.109). Quite simply, Orsino has everything to recommend him but excites Olivia in no way at all.

It is therefore necessary that Olivia be awakened to love. It is too easy for her to withdraw into the private world of her great house. We know she runs this well (IV,iii,16–20), but this shadowy life is insufficient. Olivia is both beautiful and young. It is her duty to love, marry and have children.

Olivia's discovery of love is sudden, painful and, to the audience, comic. She moves from one illusion to another: from withdrawal from the world, to love of a pageboy who is in fact a girl in disguise. We never wholly lose sight of the comedy of this, but we must realize that the comedy is overshadowed by both suffering and poetry. Orsino enjoys the languorous excesses of love; Olivia feels their sharp alternations of hope and despair.

Viola, dressed as Cesario, rouses Olivia. Her forthrightness as she delivers Orsino's declaration of love forces Olivia to pay attention to what she believes is a young pageboy. In Act I Scene v, while there is much conventional love talk, Viola's 'rudeness' excites Olivia's interest and the kindling of her love becomes clearer as she asks more and more questions. Viola herself, of course, is trying to describe the nature of Orsino's love, and by the end of the scene she is doing this in great and poignant poetry. For Olivia, hearing what she believes to be a handsome young man saying how he would woo Olivia were he in Orsino's place is deeply exciting. Left to herself, she recognizes the onset of love (I,v,278–87).

From being the remote lady she becomes the woman brave enough to risk compromising herself by sending a messenger with a ring after Cesario and begging him to return. Viola realizes immediately what has happened and sees very clearly the ludicrous position in which Olivia is placed, but she is sent by Orsino to woo Olivia again. She is granted a private audience in the garden and it is clear that the once secluded Olivia is becoming the desperate lover.

Olivia's desperation is important. We see very clearly that she is no longer remote and cold. The 'plague' she has caught makes her feverish and impulsive. She wonders how far she has compromised herself by sending the ring (III,i,108–14) and when Viola, realizing perfectly well the depth of Olivia's sudden love, says that she pities her, Olivia grasps this as a sign of hope. This has something of the irrational clutching after straws that Orsino showed in the opening scene.

Pained and irrational behaviour characterizes Olivia in love. Now it is her turn to beg, court and be rebuked, to rouse contempt in a lover. She struggles with all this bravely and beautifully. To be sure, the situation is absurd, but consider Olivia's long aside (III,i,142–53). Here, surely, is all the poetry of love; something sublime that stems from an absurd situation. We may laugh, but we cannot help being moved.

When we next see Olivia, love is nearing fever-pitch. She has sent for Cesario yet again and awaits him in a state of high expectation. That the would-be lover who first greets her is Malvolio makes him look particularly absurd, but the mention of his madness does at least allow Olivia to see that she also is suffering the insanity of love.

It is with the arrival of Sebastian that things not only become most absurd but also begin to sort themselves out. We have seen that Olivia's sudden love is strong, beautiful, poetic and richly absurd. This absurdity becomes greater when, like all the other characters, she is unable to distinguish Viola from Sebastian. When she finds the man she thinks she's in love with about to duel with Sir Toby and rushes in to save him, she thinks she has saved her future husband. At last her chance has come. She rushes Sebastian (whom she thinks is Cesario) back to her house and then, in no time at all, to a priest. Sebastian has no idea of what is going on, but he is not a young man to miss out on the main chance and he willingly accepts Olivia's love. Olivia, desperately and melodramatically in love, seems finally assured of getting her man. We laugh, naturally; but what we laugh at is a woman pushed by love to the limits of reason, a woman who has braved all.

In the last Act absurdity is taken a degree further when Cesario rushes off to apparent death at the hands of Orsino, and once again Olivia believes she has lost her man. This being a comedy, however, 'her own adventures must have a happy ending. The truth is revealed. Sebastian and Viola clasp each other, brother and sister reunited. Sebastian the male twin, is indeed Olivia's betrothed. Throughout the reunion Olivia says almost nothing. On stage, she must watch the revelation in all but silent amazement. Olivia, the woman who at the start refused to love, has won her man through a series of absurd reverses and illusions. It is perhaps appropriate that she should be silent here and give her attention to sorting out Malvolio. What we have seen in her is a woman who, through farce, pain and poetry has won her husband. He is a different man from the Orsino who courted her at the start; nonetheless she can, with appropriate dignity and bearing, suggest the double marriage of herself to the Sebastian she loves and

Orsino to the woman he now truly loves. Harmony and peace are at last restored.

SEBASTIAN

Sebastian's main role in the play is as Viola's twin brother, which adds richly to the confusion of the plot and helps bring about its solution. The fact that he and Viola are so frequently confused leads to many amusing incidents. It is also crucial that he can step in for Cesario at the end and so become Olivia's husband.

Because he is so important to the mechanics of the plot, it is unfair to dismiss Sebastian simply as an adventurer, a young man who readily agrees to marry Olivia when she virtually forces him to. Shakespeare portrays Sebastian as a much deeper character than this. Because the plot does not demand that he be shown as a true and sincere lover, he is given some depth of personality as Antonio's staunch and loyal friend.

At the start of the second Act we see Sebastian as a handsome and sensitive young man. He loves his sister, he wants to spare his friend. He is grateful, however, when Antonio does follow him and shows the depth of his feelings for him. He is ready to fight with Sir Toby, he is even more ready to fall in with Olivia's plans. His utter amazement and sense of rapture at her behaviour are both sophisticated and very funny. In Act IV Scene iii, where he is trying to puzzle out recent events, he is shown again to be sensitive and intelligent, a man of his word who swears he 'ever will be true', and probably means it.

ANTONIO

Antonio is Sebastian's sworn friend; and the Elizabethans placed a very high value on friendship. At its best it ran deep and was full of feeling.

It is clear all the way through *Twelfth Night* that Antonio is deeply fond of Sebastian, to the point, indeed, where he is prepared to risk his life for him. Like the others in the play who can love deeply, Antonio is impulsive and compassionate and experiences personal difficulties and humiliation. He is not a figure of great importance except in the mechanics of the plot (it is vital that he should confuse Viola dressed as Cesario for Sebastian, for example) but he is also someone for Sebastian to talk to and thereby tell the audience more about himself.

SIR TOBY BELCH

Sir Toby Belch is a link between the aristocrats and the low-life characters: he is a huge, rumbustious, earthy figure, a knight who gets drunk with the servants. His size alone should make him a figure of fun, but his energy, gusto and delight in helping plot Malvolio's downfall and the duel between Viola and Sir Andrew Aguecheek make him a gloriously comic figure.

Sir Toby is also a liar; he swindles Sir Andrew, and he organizes anarchic pranks. He lacks the refinement of an aristocrat. He speaks prose, not verse – but such prose! His phrases have all the earthy inventiveness of his personality, the punch and vigour of the man who, if he is broadly comic, is also much more than this.

We have noted that in *Twelfth Night* comedy and deep feeling always run close together. Sir Toby's contribution is no exception. Of course, comedy predominates. His overwhelming presence is as a rolling drunkard. As such, he stands in vital contrast to the other aristocrats: with them, we are more inclined to smile than laugh; with Sir Toby we laugh outright. What an impossible hothouse Illyria would be if we never saw Sir Toby and life below stairs! Nonetheless, Toby Belch provides more than simple contrast.

He is not on stage at the end but we understand that, as with all the lovers, he too is to be married. Fabian tells us that Sir Toby has married Maria as a reward for her successful gulling of Malvolio (V,i,360–62).

We learn at the start of the play that he is fond of her. However, where the aristocrats express their love in refined language, Sir Toby's is more earthy but, in its way, no less poetic. 'She's a beagle true bred', he says of Maria (II,iii,172). This is not the language of Orsino, but the vigorous phraseology implies an affection of which Orsino is probably incapable.

Like the other lovers, Sir Toby is touched by melancholy; he also enjoys music. But it is boisterous music that he really enjoys, the 'catch' or 'round song' that brings Malvolio from his bed. The song has also woken Maria who reprimands Sir Toby in no uncertain terms for the noise he and his friends are making. Theirs is not the language of grace, restraint or tact. Maria in particular has her feet very firmly on the ground, and she can run Sir Toby a close second with vigorous language.

Their affectionate, knockabout courtship is brought to a head through the plot to humiliate Malvolio. Notice that, just as if is Viola who is a more steadfast lover than Orsino, and Olivia who takes the initiative in wooing Cesario, so the taunting of Malvolio is largely set up by Maria. She and Sir Toby are finally united in a common cause, that of leading Malvolio into a trap of his own making.

Anarchic, knockabout comedy is an essential part of Sir Toby's personality. On the first and last occasions we see him he has been drinking, and throughout the play he threatens the well-ordered running of Olivia's household. His carousing with Sir Andrew Aguecheek is perhaps not too serious, but the baiting of Malvolio is.

The trick played on Malvolio is the revenge of ordinary, if excessively high-spirited people on a stiff and formal prig. In the garden scene at least we side with them and enjoy the bright comedy of Sir Toby's ill-contained indignation. We see too that he is a sensitive man: he does not stay long at the baiting of Malvolio, by Feste, in his madman's cell.

The duel with Viola – and later with Sebastian, who is mistaken for her – tell us a great deal about Sir Toby. First and most obviously it shows his delight in the absurd, in rumbustious trickery. The matter of the challenge, however, shows us something it is easy to overlook in Sir Toby's character: if he is comic, he is not a fool. Despite the drinking, the swaggering and the occasional bouts of melancholy, Sir Toby is an artful and intuitive man. This is essential, for he is, in modern terminology, something of a confidence man. He knows that Olivia will never marry Orsino (I,iii,103–5). He knows even better that she will not even look at Sir Andrew Aguecheek, but he still persuades the knight to stay on and so pay for their drinking bouts. He knows that the challenge Sir Andrew pens shows him to be a complete fool and that if the duel is to work at all then he must set it up himself. And finally, by a wonderful pardox, it is partly through Sir Toby that Olivia marries Sebastian. Both Sir Toby and Olivia mistake Sebastian for Viola dressed as Cesario and Sir Toby even draws his sword on him. Olivia rushes in to see, as she believes, her anarchic kinsman threatening death to the man she loves (IV,i,44). She sweeps Sebastian away to her tender care and a hasty proposal of marriage.

The last we see of Sir Toby is the drunkard limping in wounded after his confrontation with Sebastian. He cuts rather a pathetic figure among so many happy characters. He belongs too much to the low life to join them all at the end, but we gain some satisfaction from the final report of his marriage. The old drunken reprobate – earthy, lively and ultimately wholly forgivable – helps to anchor *Twelfth Night* in a recognizable and real world. Sir Toby is a liability, but we applaud his gusto and take his side against the over-refined and the priggish. He calls on Feste for a love song (II,iii,35) and it is this, with all its excesses, that Sir Toby lives for: a life of 'cakes and ale' and, finally, of married love.

MARIA

She's a beagle true bred.
(II,iii,172)

Maria is a shrewd woman of the world with a practical view of life. At Olivia's maid she perfectly complements her mistress in an easy and trusting relationship. She is also unquestionably loyal and has genuine affection for Olivia.

It is as a serving-maid that we see Maria in her true light. In her own surroundings she is a match for anyone. We first meet her reprimanding Sir Toby Belch, a man way above her station but, as she also knows, a man set in the same mould. Her language towards him is vigorous but affectionate, with none of the subtle innuendoes of the aristocracy. She is both a realist and a lover of life. She enjoys showing up Sir Andrew Aguecheek for the fool he is; and she even demonstrates that she knows more about the ways of love, even from a man's point of view, than he could ever know.

It is Maria's zest for life and her utter refusal to kowtow to Malvolio that finally kindle Sir Toby's love for her. Perhaps she knows this. She joins Feste and the two knights in their desire for revenge on Malvolio, but when they can think of nothing more imaginative than a duel, Maria suggests forging the letter from Olivia (II,iii,148–54). She plans revenge for all of them, and, as she abets Sir Toby's delight in frolics, she also wins his heart. Her fondness for Sir Toby comes across clearly when she quickly silences Feste as he talks of her and the knight (I,v,27). This is a very clever dramatic device; it is realistic and it avoids the need for Maria to express high-flown emotions which, although she might feel them, would probably be ill-suited to her style. Nonetheless, her clever plot against Malvolio does win her Sir Toby's hand; she becomes the third woman in the play – with Viola and Olivia – to woo rather than be wooed by her man. The audience may gain immense satisfaction from the knowledge that Maria and Sir Toby are to be wed.

SIR ANDREW AGUECHEEK

Sir Andrew Aguecheek is introduced to us as a nincompoop and such he remains. He is too stupid to develop with other characters in the play. He is the tall, thin counterpart to fat Sir Toby Belch, comic in manner and appearance.

Much of the comedy of Sir Andrew comes from the familiar distinction in *Twelfth Night* between illusion and reality. He would like to be a great lover, a great duellist, in his eyes the qualities of a real man. In fact, he knows nothing whatsoever about love and is an out-and-out coward. He is ignorant, although Sir Toby pretends he is learned, and totally incapable of showing originality or initiative.

Perhaps we should not judge Sir Andrew too harshly, for he does provide us with a goood deal of fun, even if it is at his own expense. We are greatly amused when Maria and Sir Toby get the better of him with their wit and cunning; we are amused when he challenges Viola to a duel, for he is just as frightened as Viola, and makes an exhibition of himself.

We may see Sir Andrew as the pathetic and witless drinking companion of Sir Toby, the man who provides the money, and without being aware of it, a great deal of the entertainment. But we should not simply dismiss him as a feeble man for, in his confusion, he is both delightful and rather sad: such a combination of feelings is now commonplace in *Twelfth Night*. Sir Andrew stands no chance of success as a lover, but there is a genuine sadness about him, and even he has his melancholy part to add to the theme: 'I was adored once too.'

If he is a sad but touching character he is, in his stupidity, even a memorable character who has more to offer the play than to be an object of scorn and derision.

MALVOLIO

Much of Malvolio's character is described by his name: the Italian *mal voglio* (Shakespeare was greatly influenced by Italian comedy) can be translated as: 'I mean ill-will.'

Malvolio's dislike of Feste is clear from the moment he first speaks, but his arrogant, dismissive jibes will lead to his undoing. However, there is far more to Malvolio than a sour temper, the sort of behaviour he displays in breaking up Sir Toby's drunken rabble (Act II Scene iii), or even when he gives Viola the ring Olivia has sent after her (Act II Scene ii). Malvolio is smug, arrogant and, in his own eyes, infinitely superior to everyone. Why? Because, as Olivia shrewdly remarks, Malvolio is 'sick of self-love'. What does she mean?

We have seen that *Twelfth Night* is a play about the discovery of love (see pp. 71–4). Orsino develops from fantasizing about love to marriage; Olivia from shunning the world to fully realizing the need for someone else in her life. For Malvolio, none of this can really happen. His fantasies of his own greatness obsess him. He cannot reach out to other people, cannot share, cannot truly love. In his opinion he is the most wonderful person in the world. He loves himself, and his false illusions of his own worth make him a complete prig. Malvolio is trapped in his own vanity and his vanity makes him blind, bitter and, ultimately, a complete and almost tragic fool.

Maria is perfectly well aware of Malvolio's weakness. In Act II Scene iii she calls him a 'puritan', and for her and the audience this word implies a sour, life-denying prude. She describes him further as a 'time-pleaser', what we might in modern terminology, call a creep. She also recognizes that Malvolio is a crashing snob. Although he is a servant, he wants to be the master, 'to be Count Malvolio'.

So much absurdity and illusion not only makes Malvolio look ridiculous, it also makes him fair game for those who despise him. As Maria shrewdly comments: 'It is his grounds of faith that all that look on him love him – and on that vice in him will my revenge find notable cause to work.' She works her revenge by playing on Malvolio's illusions. She will persuade him that Olivia is in love with him. He will be taken in by her letter and so imagine that 'greatness' is to be thrust upon him. No illusion could be greater or further from the truth. In the end, there is no more pathetic figure in the entire play.

In Act II Scene v we see Malvolio strutting towards Maria's trap. He is alone and indulging his daydreams, his illusions of wealth, power and sex. He imagines, once he is married to Olivia, how he will have his revenge on Sir Toby, the man who so roundly put him in his place in Act II Scene iii. He will indeed be 'Count Malvolio'. When he finds the letter it seems as if his daydreams have come true. Olivia, it appears, really is in love with him. Because Malvolio has no sense of humour or reality, he cannot see that he is very soon going to make a fool of himself. No one in *Twelfth Night* is more deluded than Malvolio at this point and, in this illusion of love – not really love at all, but a combination of ambition, revenge and sexual desire – he will make himself look 'mad'. With Malvolio in love, we see the fraught behaviour of the other lovers reduced to caricature. Such 'madness' is something for which Malvolio will be horribly punished.

In Act III Scene iv Malvolio presents himself to Olivia dressed in his yellow stockings and cross-garters. She, meanwhile, anxiously awaits the person she really loves, and nothing could therefore be more unwelcome than the arrival of the misguided Malvolio – lecherous, smiling, the would-be lover. We laugh at him because we have come to despise him, and keenly anticipate his humiliation. Only when he is being baited by Sir Toby do we perhaps begin to see the pathos and cruelty underneath the laughter. These are feelings of which we have been constantly aware in *Twelfth Night*. Olivia suffers; Viola suffers; Malvolio is horribly humiliated. By their revenge his enemies set him up so that he makes himself look ridiculous, a parody of the mad lover, then they try to convince him that he really is mad. The joke begins to turn sour (Act IV Scene ii). There is real cruelty here; what started as a joke has perhaps been taken too far. When Feste is left alone outside Malvolio's darkened cell (IV,ii,71–128) our laughter is almost silenced. Perhaps we say with Sir Toby: 'I would we were well rid of this knavery.'

Even when Malvolio has written his letter, Feste is cruelly late and careless about delivering it (V,i,282–97) and with the last appearance of Malvolio, Shakespeare's skill – and that of any actor or director putting on a performance of the play – is severely tested. We have been amused by the conceited prig making a fool of himself. We have seen the madness of the other lovers caricatured and cruelly baited. Now Malvolio must reappear among happy and united lovers, people with whom he has nothing in common.

But he learns nothing from his ordeal. He cannot discard his illusions, for, in the end, there is no one for him to love. At this point in the play he could be tragic. He does not appear so because his bitterness does not outweigh the happiness of the other characters. On stage and in performance, his angry return provides a sufficiently sour taste to prevent the happiness of the other characters from seeming unreal or sentimental.

But Malvolio ends as he began – quite alone. He storms off vowing revenge because he is out of place among such happy lovers and cannot forgive them for what has been done to him. Do we blame him? Perhaps not. The best we can hope is that, with Fabian (V,i,353–66), we can see that there has been wrong on both sides, and then, with Orsino, that Malvolio can be entreated 'to a peace'.

FESTE

Feste is perhaps the most difficult of all the characters in the play to understand. His role in life – that of the paid fool of a great house, the man employed for his sharpness and wit – is something none of us is familiar with.

Perhaps the easiest way of understanding him is to consider his costume, his 'motley' or fool's outfit made up from odd bands of colour. Feste is made up in the same way: his character is a strange combination of some of the various moods and themes of the play. He can be raucous with Sir Toby, yet he can sing songs of exquisite and refined melancholy. He belongs in the company of the earthier characters in the play, but he can also sing a song that 'dallies with the innocence of love'. He is a fool by name, but he is neither foolish nor mad by nature. He is shrewd, observant and mocking. In other words, he is not always what he seems.

In some ways, Feste is almost a free spirit. He belongs to Olivia's house, but he seems quite at home in Orsino's court, and whenever he appears his costume reminds us of folly, of the absurdity of the people he and the audience are watching. As he himself says: 'Foolery, sir, does walk about the orb like the sun, it shines everywhere.' Feste, as a symbol of foolishness, repeats the theme of the differences between illusion and reality once more.

Regardless of the beauty of his love songs, Feste has a cruel streak. Indeed, he is by far the cruellest character in the play. He takes revenge seriously, so much so that he never forgives Malvolio. He relishes the man's downfall and taunts him mercilessly in his darkened cell. When he finally brings him pen and paper, he is deliberately callous about delivering the letter. Feste's last words in the play are those of bitter and triumphant revenge and they help drive Malvolio from the stage.

Feste's immensely complex language also hinders our understanding of the man. It is often bitter and mocking, as a fool's should be. It is also convoluted and full of riddles. Meanings shift and slide as words tumble from his mouth (see pp. 79–80).

It is right that the play should close with the melancholy song of this strange and not wholly likeable character. He has wandered through the play sometimes bitingly satirical, at other times raucous, and on one occasion with a beautiful song on his lips. He is a constant reminder of the folly of the characters with whom he is seen. He has been bitter, vengeful, even cruel. His language has been as 'fantastical' as the love we have seen in the play. Still in his motley, he sings the song that closes *Twelfth Night*, a curious and melancholy piece, which, in its bitter-sweetness, reminds us of the rare yet eternal Never-never-land we have visited and have now left behind.

FABIAN

Fabian is not a particularly important character in the play. His chief function is as the 'straight man' among the comic characters, the man who keeps us informed of events throughout the play. He tells us that he bears a grudge against Malvolio when we are first introduced to him, and, most important, it is he who at the end of the play is present to tell us of the marriage of Maria and Sir Toby, to explain that in the taunting of Malvolio there has been right and wrong on both sides, and, finally, to be sent off to 'entreat him to a peace'.

Commentary

ILLYRIA

'This is Illyria, lady.' In the second scene the Captain tells us the setting of the play, but Illyria is less a place than a state of mind; a combination of romantic love and broad farce, a world of disguise, desire, illusion, melancholy and joy, of cruelty and happiness. In Illyria we hear biting wit and word-play, and also some of the most purely beautiful of Shakespeare's poetry. The world of Illyria and *Twelfth Night* is thus a comic one, not simply because it makes us laugh, but because its confusions are brought to a happy ending. Finally, though Illyria may be a Never-never-land, it is also the place where people ultimately find true identity and true love.

LOVE

Love, as we are reminded by the opening words of the play, is the abiding theme of *Twelfth Night*. We see here an aristocrat suffering the extreme pangs of romantic passion. For him, such male ardour is ravenous, moody and inventive. It has its pains and its imagined rewards, but, above all, it is gloriously self-indulgent. For Orsino, love for Olivia is a ritual and a performance. His ardour is mightily high-flown and it leads to some magnificent poetry, but it has its measure of absurdity. Orsino's bouts of self-indulgence are frankly overdone, and we may begin to wonder if he considers Olivia a real woman, or some creature hallowed in his imagination. Ultimately we realize that

Orsino is in love with the idea of love. He is fascinated by the suffering, the poetry and the techniques of courtship. He even goes so far as to force the woman who loves him – and to whose true feelings and identity he is blind – to do his wooing for him. The game of love is all. His lady exists most readily in his mind's eye. When he actually encounters Olivia (Act 5 Scene i) he learns that his 'sovereign cruelty' is engaged to another man. Orsino's game of love is suddenly over. His passion thwarted, he threatens to kill Viola (there is real danger in such passion as his), but when he learns that Viola is really a woman, he marries her without delay. Such a complete *volte face* only emphasizes and makes more comic the absurdity of his extreme male ardour. Like all of the illusions in the play, Orsino's false love rapidly crumbles, to be replaced by true love.

Paradoxically, Olivia is like Orsino, the man she will not marry: she too has let illusion and excess – her excessive and unnatural mourning for a dead brother and father – stand in the way of true love. Her coming to terms with reality and love is, however, far more complicated than Orsino's. As we watch Olivia suddenly change from the woman who has denied herself warmth and human affection and become the desperate wooer of Cesario, we may be glad at her change of heart, but we can also be highly amused. Olivia does not realize that she has merely exchanged one illusion for another: the self-denying love for a dead brother and father with love for a woman disguised as a man. The situation is absurd but touching. The discovery of love is, as for most people, deeply painful to Olivia. Cesario's beauty and anger hurt her (I I I,i,142–53). That her love is not reciprocated drives her to distraction. Indeed, there is about Olivia's love something of the madness that touches all the leading characters in the play.

Olivia finds her way out of this world of pain and illusion through the most absurd comedy. The fact that Sebastian is a man and all but identical to Viola allows Olivia to marry him with hardly a second thought. If this is laughable, Olivia is not simply a figure of fun. She experiences for the first time the pain of love, and in doing so elicits the audience's sympathy.

The purest love in the play is that of Viola for Orsino. Her love for him is constant, deep and selfless, and in this she differs from most of the other major characters. Her love for Orsino becomes the guiding star of her life. For him she will do anything, far more than sing or entertain him, which is what she at first proposed. With almost no thought for herself or her own happiness, Viola willingly suffers the humiliation of paying court to another woman in the name of the man she adores. And she does not baulk at the task. As she describes the passion of the man she loves to another woman, she rises to the heights of poetry (I,v,257–65). Dressed as Cesario, she is caught in the difficult but comic position of being loved by Olivia. She is also abused by Sir Andrew Aguecheek. Finally, when Orsino is rebuffed by Olivia face to face, discovers she is married and threatens to kill the person he is next fond of – Viola disguised as Cesario – Viola willingly offers to die. Only at the end, when all the illusions are played out, does Viola promise to reveal herself as a woman and, in so doing, win her master's hand in marriage.

For Shakespeare, marriage is the great reality. In it, love, affection and reason combine, just as they have always combined in the character of Viola. Her love for Orsino is more real than his for Olivia. She mourns more truly for her brother than does Olivia for hers. She is naturally and honestly affectionate. It is, in the circumstances, only right that she should marry the man upon whom she has lavished so much secret love, and take up her position as: 'Orsino's mistress, and his fancy's queen'.

Her brother Sebastian does not have such weighty and important things to do. Indeed, he is a lesser character altogether. When he comes to Illyria – the land of love and illusion – he discovers a race of apparently mad people. However, when a rich and beautiful aristocrat declares herself passionately in love with him he is not one to miss the main chance. He willingly returns Olivia's affection – if not as deeply as it is offered – and plays along with good grace, so that at the end he has attained as much happiness as the others, but at far less cost to himself.

The most foolish lover, of course, is Sir Andrew Aguecheek. He comes to Illyria to court Olivia: but he is swindled – he needs to marry

Olivia to recoup his losses – wounded in a fight and thoroughly humiliated. We cannot take Sir Andrew at all seriously as a lover, nor really as anything else. However, as befits the melancholy in the play, he has one sad line: 'I was adored once, too.' And of course the way he says this makes us laugh.

The love between Maria and Sir Toby is real but not at all romantic. Although Sir Toby is a knight, he employs none of Orsino's poetry in his speech. Yet, when he calls Maria 'a beagle true bred' he is expressing genuine affection. It is an affection Feste certainly recognizes (I,v,25–6); even when Maria reprimands Sir Toby for his carousing we sense that she reciprocates his love. The trick they play on Malvolio draws them closer together and this should be apparent in a good production. After all, we learn almost at the end that it is because the trick has gone so well that Sir Toby has proposed to Maria and been accepted. They too find married love.

The Elizabethans also valued love in friendship. Antonio is the best example of one who will risk everything, including his life, to be with a friend, in this case Sebastian. This is not only touching, but it also lends depth to Sebastian's character. Because of the speed with which his affair with Olivia develops, we need to be assured that he is more than a superficial adventurer; the affection Sebastian shows Antonio when they are reunited admirably proves this.

There is one final form of love in *Twelfth Night*: self-love. This is personified in Malvolio, as Olivia makes clear to us (I,v,85–91). Extremes of self-love, like extremes of romantic love, are an absurd illusion. Malvolio falls victim to both extremes. For this, like the others, he must suffer. The madness that the others come so close to is, unlike the greatness Malvolio had hoped for, thrust upon him. And like them he suffers, but for Malvolio neither the love of a woman nor marriage is there to save him. For this reason Malvolio cannot be on the stage at the end of the play. In the depths of his illusion he has no place in the happy realities of married love.

COMEDY AND FARCE

Twelfth Night is a comedy because it has a happy ending. This, however, is insufficient. We should be aware, in our reading of the play, of the various levels at which the comedy works, and it is worth remembering that the examiners are looking for, amongst other things, your skill in perceiving and expressing understanding of these levels.

It may be easiest if we start with farce. The single purpose of farce is to make us laugh and there is much in *Twelfth Night* which is straightforwardly funny. The duel between Viola and Sir Andrew Aguecheek, or what happens to Sebastian when he arrives at Olivia's house are among the most obvious examples. We should add to these Malvolio's appearance in his nightshirt and later in his cross-gartered stockings. Such laughter as these scenes provoke is pleasant in itself. They are pure entertainment and an important part of our pleasure in the theatre.

But the laughter that such farcical scenes produce is not the only – or even the major – effect of the play. *Twelfth Night* is wise and richly poetic. If there is joy and melancholy in the play, there is, above all, self-discovery. These are more subtle and serious issues and we must be aware of them if we are fully to appreciate the range of Shakespeare's achievement. Remember that *Twelfth Night* was written in the same year as *Hamlet*, one of the most searchingly profound plays in dramatic literature. In *Hamlet*, Shakespeare presents serious issues in a serious way. In *Twelfth Night* he presents serious issues in a comic way. Thus, we find amusement in the excesses of Orsino's self-indulgence, and at the pangs of love Olivia suffers. We are nevertheless aware that Shakespeare has an important message: that romantic love may be sudden and violent. It sweeps over people. It can be painful. In the near madness of obsession, characters humiliate themselves without realizing it. Nonetheless, we sympathize with them.

It is this combination of amusement and sympathy that Shakespeare aims at through the greater part of the play. We should ask how he achieves it.

Look first at the brief synopsis of the play (pp. 11–18). From such a brief outline it is difficult to see how *Twelfth Night* could be a moving and delightful experience. Orsino is in love with a woman who rejects him. He sends his page to court her. Neither Orsino nor Olivia know that this 'boy' Cesario is in fact a woman dressed up as a man. Olivia falls in love with 'him' because she thinks he is a boy. Orsino marries 'him' when he finds she is a woman. Nothing could be more absurd, more artificial or ridiculous. Throughout the play – even in its most serious moments – we are aware of the need to laugh at it. Three things make the play serious and moving: the incomparable beauty of the poetry (as in Act I Scene v and Act II Scene iv), which is so utterly at odds with the situation that gives rise to it; the sureness of the characterization, for all of the characters are far more than puppets in a highly contrived plot; the contrast and relief offered by the low-life scenes. These three things – poetry, characterization and contrast – add much to the absurdity of plot. Our feelings become truly engaged. We pity Olivia and Viola. The depth of the feelings Shakespeare shows us is so much more than we might expect. The melancholy, bitterness and cruelty in the play are so much stronger than we might have imagined. When watching a performance of *Twelfth Night* we are always near to laughter. Sometimes we are close to tears. Perhaps this combination is nowhere more powerful than in the recognition scene between Viola and Sebastian (V,i,223–55). But it is this scene which leads to the final happiness that closes the play and which allows us to call it a comedy.

DISGUISE: ILLUSION AND REALITY

> *Disguise, I see thou art a wickedness*
> *Wherein the pregnant enemy does much.*
> (II,ii,27–8)

Viola's words take us to the heart of this theme, for much of the comic effect of the play springs from disguise in one form or another. It is obvious that the farcical element in the play – lady loves boy who is really a girl – is dependent on it. But, as we have said, *Twelfth Night* is much more than a farce.

Disguise is a form of illusion. It makes people appear to be one thing, while, in reality, they are another. How many examples of this can we find in the play? Obviously, Viola appears to be a boy and is actually a girl. To many of the characters in the play Sebastian appears to be Viola and much comedy results from this. But there are other forms of illusion besides those which fool the eye. We can call Orsino's love for Olivia an illusion. He appears to be obsessed by her. Really, he is in love with love. Olivia's excessive mourning for her brother is false. She discovers the real power of love when she meets Cesario. Even then, her passion is based on an illusion: Cesario appears to be a boy, in fact he is Viola in disguise.

One of the clearest examples of illusion in the play is the fate of Malvolio. At the beginning of Act I I Scene v we see him daydreaming. No doubt this is harmless enough. However, when Malvolio picks up Maria's letter he falls headfirst into the greatest of illusions: the belief that his daydreams have come true. In his yellow stockings and cross-garters he is the most absurd lover in the whole play. We laugh, but perhaps we should pause for thought. Is his cruelly misplaced passion so very different from Olivia's love for the 'boy' Cesario? Is his self-delusion – of himself as the great lover – much removed from Orsino's view of himself? Probably not; the difference is one of degree. We laugh out loud at Malvolio. There is no poetry here. His feelings are not hurt at this point; the pain is in his legs, caused by the tightness of his garters. Malvolio is ridiculous disguised as the lover. His love is an illusion. Only at the end of the play, when the disguises have all been seen through and illusion has vanished, do reality and true love at last rule.

MADNESS

Malvolio's belief that Olivia loves him is an illusion. It is comic, even farcical. It also tells us a great deal about the false loves of the others:

of Orsino and Olivia herself. To express it another way, the comic sub-plot comments on the main plot; it caricatures its main themes. This is usually the case with Shakespeare's sub-plots, and it is certainly so in the mad-house scene.

Malvolio's behaviour as a lover is so absurd that Sir Toby and his companions throw him into a madman's darkened cell. Love, they cruelly pretend, has driven Malvolio mad. Just as Shakespeare carica-tured the theme of love and illusion in Malvolio's courtship scene, so here he characterizes another theme from the main plot: the idea that extreme romantic passion (like Orsino's) is a sort of lunacy. It is important to realize that none of the characters is actually mad; they have simply been greatly distracted by their obsessions. They are no longer level-headed. We could not apply that adjective to the Orsino of the first scene, nor to the Orsino of the last Act whose thoughts, 'ripe in mischief', have led him to consider murdering Cesario. Such is the desperate, violent measure, so close to madness, towards which his extreme ardour leads him.

Olivia too recognizes how close to madness her love for Cesario has brought her. As she waits in a state of heightened anxiety for the arrival of Cesario, she is told of the arrival of the 'mad' Malvolio who 'does nothing but smile'. She comments (III,iv,13–14):

> *Go, call him hither. I am as mad as he*
> *If sad and merry madness equal be.*

Sebastian comments further on love and madness. Having wondered on his arrival if Olivia's household is completely mad, his further adventures only seem to confirm this. A beautiful and noble lady courts him with almost unimaginable speed and fury and at the opening of Act IV Scene iii, assuring himself that he is not dreaming all these strange events, he tells himself that in this hectic flood of passion he feels 'wonder' but 'not madness'. Nonetheless (and you should make sure you understand the very complex words (IV,iii,8–20)), he is ready to defy reason, to admit that the only probable answer to all this is that either he or Olivia is mad.

The taunting of the 'mad' Malvolio is cruel and an extreme caricature of the themes of love, farce, illusion, reality and madness. The basis of it is this: Malvolio is sane but is suffering from the illusion that Olivia loves him. Because it is to his advantage and flatters his vanity, he acts the part of the extreme romantic lover whose passion makes him appear insane. Sir Toby and the others, who realize the truth, choose to brand Malvolio as truly mad to further their revenge. In other words, they treat a sane man suffering from a mild delusion as a true lunatic. They lock him away in a darkened cell and then try to convince him, by speaking in riddles, that his cell is not dark at all. Feste, meanwhile – who plays the fool but is in fact exceptionally level-headed – disguises himself as a priest. The result of so much illusion is that Malvolio suffers greatly, and as he does so, many of the themes of the play are brought together and caricatured.

WIT

In Act III Scene i Feste describes his relationship with Olivia: 'I am indeed not her fool, but her corrupter of words' (ll. 34–5). You will have noticed how Feste manipulates the language to suit his needs. He speaks in such riddles and puns that one has to be quite sure that one understands his meaning.

Why does he use puns so much? The first and most obvious answer is that the Elizabethan audience found them funny, and jokes are obviously an essential part of comedy. The second and more complex reason is that puns are part of the theme of illusion. Where most people use words in their original, sensible, straightforward sense to express something more clearly, this is not so with Feste. When Viola asks him 'Art not thou the Lady Olivia's fool?', no question could be more direct and simple. Feste, however, interprets Viola's last word as 'foolishness' and replies with mock dignity, 'The Lady Olivia has no folly'. We, in fact, know how foolish she really is. Thus Feste plays with words, 'corrupts' them, in his own phrase. Simple words are given new meanings. Just as Viola changes her appearance, so Feste alters the meaning of words, causing confusion and chaos between appearance and reality. Like love, Feste's wit is 'high fantastical'.

MELANCHOLY AND MUSIC

> *Now the melancholy god protect thee, and the*
> *tailor make thy doublet of changeable taffeta, for thy*
> *mind is a very opal.*

(II,iv,72–4)

Feste's words point to another important theme in the play: that of melancholy (what we may loosely call sadness or depression), the extreme forms of which the Elizabethans identified with madness. (Even today we call manic depression an illness.)

There is much melancholy in *Twelfth Night* for there is much near madness in the play. Often it is enchanting and helps to account for the play's bitter-sweet taste. For example, take the scene from which the above quotation comes. It opens with a haunting description of the old days and moves on to Viola's poignant expression of her love. But it is Feste himself who provides the most beautiful and sad touch to the scene with his exquisite song, 'Come away, come away, death'. Such melancholy is rare and, when well directed, the lilt of words and music creates one of the loveliest moments in all drama. We are given a view of a very precious, lovely, fragile and lonely world.

Music often accompanies melancholy in the play and Feste's final song is a further example of this. As an epilogue, it reinforces the ideal of the sadly poetic, melancholy other-worldliness of Illyria.

SELF-DISCOVERY

Twelfth Night ends, as a comedy must, on an almost entirely happy note. The lovers are united. Orsino and Viola, Olivia and Sebastian,

Maria and Sir Toby. Sir Andrew has faded from our minds. Only Malvolio has refused to remain on stage. He has stormed off, vowing vengeance, but it is hoped that he will be persuaded to return to the harmonious group (V,i,377). Malvolio alone is an outcast. He had not found the truth the others have, a truth of happiness based on love, founded on marriage. It is towards this that the whole play has been working. Married love is the final and greatest reality.

To reach it, the characters have had to throw off illusion. Orsino has had to discard his excesses of emotion, Olivia has had to experience real love for a living person and then secure it. Viola, whose love has been pure and true throughout the play, is at last able to throw off her disguise when the others have, in turn, discarded their own illusions.

Malvolio cannot find himself in this journey from illusion to reality. Trapped in the maze of his self-love, he has much to learn. As always, he throws the themes of the play into sharp relief. Like the others, he is stripped of his illusion, but, unlike them, there is no love waiting for him once his foolishness had been exposed. For them, but not for Malvolio, self-discovery ends in happiness and harmony. Perhaps he will be wooed back to the fold, but it is with characters who have learned to know themselves, who are happy, united and wiser from the experience, that the play ends.

Examination Questions

1. Viola has been described as Shakespeare's most attractive heroine. What attractive qualities do you find in her character? Illustrate by quotation and close references from the play.

(Associated Examining Board, 1970)

2. By careful reference to specific scenes in the play, show how mistaken identity adds to the humour and excitement.

(Associated Examining Board, 1970)

3. 'Although Feste, the Clown, takes little or no part in the development of the plot, he is an important character.' Discuss.

(Associated Examining Board, 1970)

4. Choose one of the following passages and answer the questions below it.

Either
(i)

OLIVIA: 'What is your parentage?'
         'Above my fortunes, yet my state is well:
         I am a gentleman.' I'll be sworn thou art:
         Thy tongue, thy face, thy limbs, actions, and spirit,
         Do give thee five-fold blazon. Not too fast: 5
                        soft! soft!

        Unless the master were the man. How now!
        Even so quickly may one catch the plague?
        Methinks I feel this youth's perfections
        With an invisible and subtle stealth   10
        To creep in at mine eyes. Well, let it be.
        What, ho! Malvolio!

(a)   Whose words does Olivia quote in line 1, and whose reply in lines 2 and 3? What was the purpose of this person's conversation with Olivia?

(b)   Give the substance of the words spoken by this person just before taking leave of Olivia.

(c)   What instructions does Olivia now give to Malvolio?

(d)   Give in your own words the meaning of 'five-fold blazon' (l.5), and the full significance of 'Even so quickly may one catch the plague?' (l.8).

Or
(ii)

SIR   He is knight dubbed with unhatched rapier, and on
TOBY: carpet consideration; but he is a devil in private brawl.
        Souls and bodies hath he divorced three; and his
        incensement at this moment is so implacable that
        satisfaction can be none but by pangs of death and   5
        sepulchre. Hob, nob, is his word: give't or take't.

(a)   To whom is Sir Toby speaking and about whom? What is he trying to arrange for them to do?

(b)   Give the substance of the reply made by the person to whom Sir Toby is speaking.

(c)   Give in your own words the meaning of (i) unhatched (l.1), (ii) on carpet consideration (l.2), and (iii) incensement (l.4).

(d)   Who else is present during this conversation? How does he describe the person about whom Sir Toby is speaking in the above passage?

   (e)   On his next appearance Sir Toby gives a misleading description of his encounter with the person to whom he is speaking in the above passage. Give the substance of this description.

5. 'He hath been most notoriously abused'. Give a clear account of the plot against Malvolio, and explain to what extent you think he deserved the treatment he received during the play.

6. Write accounts of two occasions on which Viola woos Olivia on Orsino's behalf, showing what impressions you have gained from these episodes of the character of Olivia.

7. Referring to their speeches and actions, bring out the contrasts between Sir Toby Belch and Sir Andrew Aguecheek.

(University of London Examination Board, 1971)

1. Choose one of the following passages and answer the questions below it:

Either
(i)

MARIA: The devil a puritan that he is, or anything constantly
           but a time-pleaser; an affectioned ass, that cons
           state without book, and utters it by great swarths:
           the best persuaded of himself; so crammed, as he
           thinks, with excellences, that it is his ground of faith   5
           that all who look on him love him; and on that vice in
           him will my revenge find notable cause to work.

   (a)   Who else is present when Maria speaks these words? About whom is she speaking?
   (b)   What has just happened to cause her to say these words?
   (c)   Explain in your own words the form Maria's revenge is to take as suggested by her in her next speech.

(d) Give in your own words the meaning of (i) affectioned (l.2), and (ii) cons state without book and utters it by great swarths (ll.2–3).

(e) What do the other characters present during this speech say of Maria after she has left them?

Or
(ii)

SEBASTIAN: I am sorry, madam, I have hurt your kinsman:
But, had it been the brother of my blood,
I must have done no less with wit and safety.
You throw a strange regard upon me, and by that
I do perceive it hath offended you: 5
Pardon me, sweet one, even for the vows
We made each other but so late ago.

(a) To whom is Sebastian speaking? Who is the kinsman (l.1)? What has Sebastian done to him?

(b) Give in your own words the meaning of (i) with wit and safety (l.3), and (ii) you throw a strange regard upon me (l.4).

(c) What are the vows (l.6)? State briefly how they came to be made.

(d) Give briefly the immediate reactions of (i) Orsino and (ii) Antonio to Sebastian's speech and his appearance on the scene.

2. 'A comedy should begin in trouble, end in joy and be centred in love.' By referring closely to events of the play, show how true you consider this statement to be of *Twelfth Night*.

3. Give a clear account of the scene in which Malvolio finds and reads the letter, bringing out the full humour of the episode.

4. Explain why Sir Andrew challenges Cesario and give an account of the difficulties he encounters as a result, showing what aspects of his character are revealed as he grapples with the difficulties.

(*University of London Examination Board, 1972*)

1. Read the following passage and answer the questions below it.

DUKE:	Cesario,
	Thou know'st no less but all; I have unclasp'd
	To thee the book even of my secret soul:
	Therefore, good youth, address thy gait unto her,
	Be not denied access, stand at her doors, 5
	And tell them, there thy fixed foot shall grow
	Till thou have audience.
VIOLA:	Sure, my noble lord,
	If she be so abandon'd to her sorrow
	As it is spoke, she never will admit me. 10
DUKE:	Be clamorous and leap all civil bounds
	Rather than make unprofited return.
VIOLA:	Say I do speak with her, my lord, what then?
DUKE:	O! then unfold the passion of my love;
	Surprise her with discourse of my dear faith: 15
	It shall become thee well to act my woes;
	She will attend it better in thy youth
	Than in a nuncio of more grave aspect.
VIOLA:	I think not so, my lord.
DUKE:	Dear lad, believe it; 20
	For they shall yet belie thy happy years
	That say thou art a man: Diana's lip
	Is not more smooth and rubious; thy small pipe
	Is as the maiden's organ, shrill and sound;
	And all is semblative a woman's part. 25
	I know thy constellation is right apt

> For this affair. Some four or five attend him;
> All, if you will; for I myself am best
> When least in company. Prosper well in this,
> And thou shalt live as freely as thy lord, 30
> To call his fortunes thine.

VIOLA: I'll do my best
> To woo your lady.

(a) How do the first three lines of the above passage confirm what Valentine has said to Cesario just before the Duke's arrival? Give an account of the reports of Cesario's actions a little later in the play which show that she heeds the instructions given to her in ll.5–7 and l.11.

(b) Give a concise account of Cesario's attempt to carry out the Duke's instructions in ll. 14, 15. Is his prediction in ll.16–18 fulfilled?

(c) What do you learn of Orsino's character and mood from the given passage? Support each point you make by referring to the relevant details from the passage.

(d) Explain clearly what the Duke means in ll.21–4, and show how his words are an example of dramatic irony. Give the comment of Viola (not quoted above) which ends the scene, bringing out the full irony of her situation.

2. 'Olivia, Malvolio and Sir Andrew are all self-deceived as well as being deceived by others.' Show how this statement is true of any two of these three characters in the play, and indicate briefly to what extent each of the two you discuss has become wiser at the end of it.

3. Bringing out the full humour of each episode, give concise accounts of the episodes in which (a) Malvolio finds and reads the letter forged by Maria, and (b) he appears before Olivia carrying out the letter's instructions.

(*University of London Examination Board, 1972*)

4. Read the following passage and answer the questions below it.

MALVOLIO: 'Tis but fortune: all is fortune. Maria once told me she did affect me; and I have heard herself come thus near, that should she fancy, it should be one of my complexion. Besides, she uses me with a more exalted respect than anyone else that follows her. What should I think on't?

SIR TOBY: Here's an over-weening rogue!

FABIAN: O, peace! Contemplation makes a rare turkey-cock of him: how he jets under his advanced plumes!

SIR ANDREW: 'Slight, I could so beat the rogue!

SIR TOBY: Peace! I say.

MALVOLIO: To be Count Malvolio!

SIR TOBY: Ah, rogue!

SIR ANDREW: Pistol him, pistol him.

SIR TOBY: Peace! peace!

MALVOLIO: There is example for't: the lady of the Strachy married the yeoman of the wardrobe.

SIR ANDREW: Fie on him, Jezebel!

FABIAN: O, peace! now he's deeply in; look how imagination blows him.

MALVOLIO: Having been three months married to her, sitting in my state, –

SIR TOBY: O! for a stone-bow, to hit him in the eye!

MALVOLIO: Calling my officers about me, in my branched velvet gown; having come from a day-bed, where I have left Olivia sleeping, –

SIR TOBY: Fire and brimstone!

(a)   What do you learn of Malvolio's state of mind from what he says in the above passage and from what Maria has said, just before he appeared, about his behaviour?

(b)   What does Malvolio go on to say about Sir Toby and Sir Andrew? What do the reactions and remarks of the two knights, from Malvolio's entrance to the end of the scene, reveal of their characters?

(c)   Show, by close reference to Malvolio's speeches and actions in earlier scenes, how his behaviour in the scene from which the passage is taken is consistent with what we already know of his character.

5. 'Shakespeare presents love in rich variety.' By close reference to the play, show that many different kinds of love are presented in *Twelfth Night*.

6. Traditionally, in the merrymaking of Twelfth Night the general order of things is overturned. Show, by reference to several examples, how this topsy-turvydom is presented in *Twelfth Night*.

(*University of London Examination Board, 1973*)

MORE ABOUT PENGUINS, PELICANS AND PUFFINS

For further information about books available from Penguins please write to Dept EP, Penguin Books Ltd, Harmondsworth, Middlesex UB7 0DA.

In the U.S.A.: For a complete list of books available from Penguins in the United States write to Dept DG, Penguin Books, 299 Murray Hill Parkway, East Rutherford, New Jersey 07073.

In Canada: For a complete list of books available from Penguins in Canada write to Penguin Books Canada Ltd, 2801 John Street, Markham, Ontario L3R 1B4.

In Australia: For a complete list of books available from Penguins in Australia write to the Marketing Department, Penguin Books Australia Ltd, P.O. Box 257, Ringwood, Victoria 3134.

In New Zealand: For a complete list of books available from Penguins in New Zealand write to the Marketing Department, Penguin Books (N.Z.) Ltd, P.O. Box 4019, Auckland 10.

In India: For a complete list of books available from Penguins in India write to Penguin Overseas Ltd, 706 Eros Apartments, 56 Nehru Place, New Delhi 110019.

Penguin Passnotes

Carefully tailored to the requirements of the main examination boards (for O-level or CSE exams), Penguin Passnotes are an invaluable companion to your studies.

Covering a wide range of English literature texts as well as many other subjects, Penguin Passnotes will include:

English Literature

A Man for All Seasons
Chaucer: General Prologue
Cider With Rosie
Great Expectations
Jane Eyre
Pride and Prejudice

Silas Marner
The Mayor of Casterbridge
The Woman in White
To Kill a Mockingbird
Wuthering Heights

including
Shakespeare

As You Like It
Henry IV, Part I
Julius Caesar
Macbeth

The Merchant of Venice
Twelfth Night
Romeo and Juliet

and
Other Areas

Biology
Chemistry
Economics
English Language
French
Geography

Modern World History
Physics
Human Biology
Mathematics
Modern Mathematics

Penguin Examination Bestsellers

Plus fully annotated editions of your set texts in
the New Penguin Shakespeare